The Gingerbread Golem Grimoire

The Gingerbread Golem Grimoire

Matthew Petchinsky

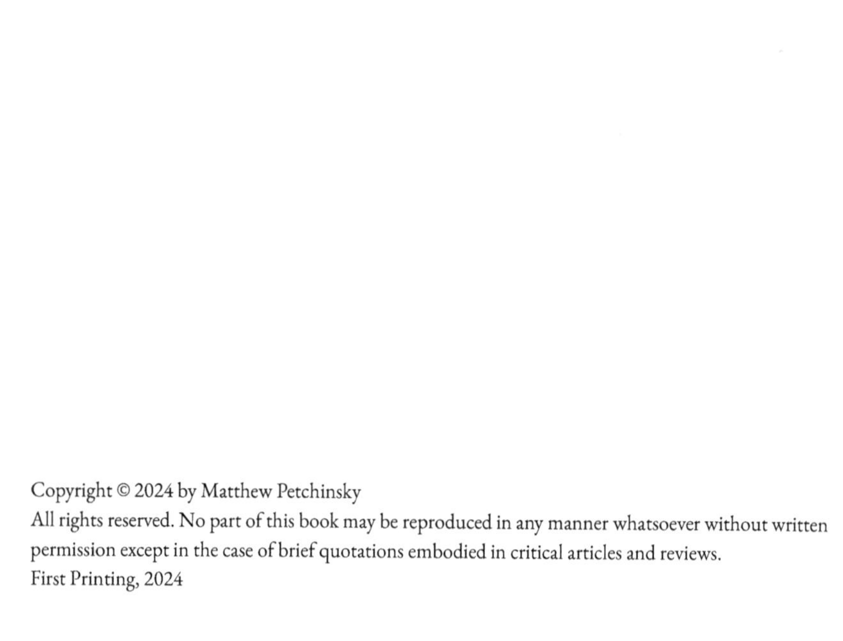

The Gingerbread Golem Grimoire: Sweet Magicks and Spells for the Festive Witch
By: Matthew Petchinsky

Introduction: The Sweet Origins of the Gingerbread Golem

The holiday season has long been a time of warmth, wonder, and magic. Among the flickering lights, fragrant evergreens, and the soft glow of candle flames, a guardian rises from an unexpected source: the humble gingerbread. But this isn't just a charming cookie; it is something far more profound. Welcome to the enchanted world of the **Gingerbread Golem**, a figure of sweetness and strength, steeped in folklore and magic.

The Folklore of the Gingerbread Golem

The origins of the Gingerbread Golem trace back through centuries of myth and tradition. Rooted in the concept of the golem—a protective entity crafted from earth or clay in Jewish mysticism—this festive counterpart takes on a softer, sweeter form. As tales traveled across cultures, the idea of animating an inanimate figure with purpose and magic evolved. In European traditions, gingerbread itself gained symbolic status as a festive treat and a medium for storytelling, decorated intricately to ward off evil and bring joy.

The Gingerbread Golem, however, is more than a confection. It embodies protection, guidance, and a sense of community. Some legends speak of villagers who crafted enchanted gingerbread figures to guard their homes during the darkest nights of winter, while others tell of magical gingerbread beings that guided lost travelers through snowy forests.

The Gingerbread Golem, with its aromatic blend of spices and its sturdy yet edible form, represents the fusion of strength and sweetness. It serves as a reminder that power need not always be harsh and that even in the toughest times, warmth and kindness can protect and guide us.

Symbolism: Sweetness, Strength, and Spirit

At its core, the Gingerbread Golem is a symbol of balance. Its sweetness represents kindness, compassion, and the nurturing aspect of magic, while its structure—a solid creation baked to perfection—symbolizes resilience and protection. Together, these qualities make the Gingerbread Golem a perfect figure for those seeking both magical guidance and steadfast defense.

- **Spices as Symbols:** Ginger, cinnamon, nutmeg, and cloves are not just ingredients but also magical allies. Each brings its own protective, healing, or energizing properties to the Gingerbread Golem.
- **The Circle of Creation:** The process of crafting a Gingerbread Golem—from mixing and shaping the dough to baking and decorating—represents the cycle of manifestation in magical practice. It teaches us patience, focus, and the importance of intention.
- **Edibility and Unity:** Unlike traditional golems made of clay, the Gingerbread Golem is meant to be shared. Consuming it during rituals or family gatherings strengthens communal bonds and reinforces the magic imbued within.

The Gingerbread Golem as Protector and Guide

The Gingerbread Golem steps into two critical roles: protector and guide. In its protective role, it stands as a barrier against negativity, malevolence, and harm. Placing a Gingerbread Golem in your home can serve as a magical sentinel, warding off ill intentions and keeping your space safe.

As a guide, the Gingerbread Golem assists in navigating life's uncertainties, especially during the hectic and often chaotic holiday season. Through rituals and spells outlined in this book, the Golem can become a spiritual companion, offering clarity and wisdom when you need it most.

- **Protection:** Gingerbread Golems are particularly effective at creating energetic shields around your home, family, or workspace. Their sweet scent and symbolic nature make them ideal for fostering peace and security.
- **Guidance:** Whether you're seeking answers through divination or simply looking for a magical ally to assist you in decision-making, the Gingerbread Golem is there to lend its sugary wisdom.

What You'll Find in This Grimoire

This book is more than a collection of recipes and spells; it is an invitation to embrace the magic of the Gingerbread Golem and infuse your holidays with its enchanted presence. Through carefully crafted rituals, recipes, and crafts, you will learn how to connect with this festive figure and bring its protective and guiding energies into your life.

Here's what to expect:

- **Part I: Crafting Your Connection to the Gingerbread Golem** – Dive into the process of creating and animating your Golem, exploring its symbolism and how to establish a magical bond.
- **Part II: Sweet Spells and Festive Rituals** – Learn practical spells and rituals for protection, harmony, and manifestation, using the Golem as your magical focal point.
- **Part III: Magical Crafts and Seasonal Enchantments** – Discover enchanting ways to incorporate the Gingerbread Golem into your holiday decorations and traditions.
- **Part IV: Advanced Gingerbread Magicks** – Delve into more complex rituals and techniques, from creating gingerbread familiars to seasonal portal magic.
- **Part V: Honoring and Preserving the Golem's Spirit** – Explore how to keep your connection to the Golem alive, repair its energy, and honor its legacy beyond the holiday season.

Additionally, the **appendices** provide:

- A detailed list of magical properties for the ingredients and tools used throughout the book.
- Templates for sigils, chants, and other aids to enhance your rituals.

A Sweet Beginning

As you embark on this magical journey, remember that the Gingerbread Golem is more than a holiday tradition—it is a symbol of hope, strength, and connection. Whether you are new to magical practice or a seasoned witch, this grimoire will guide you in working with this sweet yet powerful ally. Together, let us awaken the spirit of the Gingerbread Golem and bring its warmth and magic into our lives.

May your path be sweet and your spells strong. Let the journey begin!

Part I: Crafting Your Connection to the Gingerbread Golem

Chapter 1: The Spirit of Sweetness

The Gingerbread Golem is far more than a whimsical holiday creation. At its heart lies the **Spirit of Sweetness**, a profound and magical essence that serves as the foundation of its protective and guiding nature. Sweetness, in both taste and symbolism, carries a unique magical vibration. It soothes, nurtures, and fortifies, forming the cornerstone of this enchanting figure's power.

Understanding the Essence of the Gingerbread Golem

To truly connect with the Gingerbread Golem, one must first understand its essence: a balance of sweetness, strength, and spirit.

1. Sweetness as a Core Attribute

Sweetness represents the nurturing aspect of magic. It invites joy, comfort, and community—qualities essential for protection and guidance. The Gingerbread Golem embodies this sweetness in both form and function, making it a potent symbol of festive magic.

- **Sweetness as Energy:** The sugary components of the Golem—molasses, honey, and spices—are not merely ingredients but carriers of positive energy. They attract abundance, repel bitterness, and foster harmony in the spaces they inhabit.
- **Alchemy in Baking:** The process of transforming simple ingredients into a Gingerbread Golem mirrors the alchemical process in magic. By combining elements with intention, you create a vessel capable of holding and channeling protective energies.

2. Strength Beneath the Sweetness

While sweetness is its outer layer, the Gingerbread Golem's essence is fortified by an underlying strength. This strength is not harsh or aggressive but rather a quiet resilience that stands firm against negativity. Like the structural integrity of a well-baked gingerbread figure, the Golem's energy is grounded and enduring.

- **Symbolism of Sturdiness:** The Golem's physical form, baked to perfection, symbolizes its role as a steadfast guardian. A well-made Gingerbread Golem does not crumble under pressure, just as its magical energy remains strong in the face of challenges.

The Power of Sweetness as Magical Protection

Sweetness in magic is often overlooked in favor of more aggressive protective measures. Yet, sweetness carries its own potent form of defense. It disarms negativity, diffuses conflict, and creates an environment where harm cannot thrive. In the context of the Gingerbread Golem, sweetness becomes a shield that guards without causing harm.

1. Sweetness as a Disarming Force

Negative energies often thrive in environments of fear, anger, or tension. Sweetness counters these energies by replacing them with positivity and calm.

- **Diffusing Conflict:** The presence of sweetness can transform the emotional energy of a space. A Gingerbread Golem, imbued with sweet magic, acts as a mediator, reducing tension and fostering peace.
- **Repelling Negativity:** Just as sugar wards off bitterness in flavor, it can symbolically repel bitterness in life. The sweetness of the Golem creates a magical barrier that shields against ill intentions and negative influences.

2. Sweetness as an Attraction for Positivity

Sweetness not only protects but also attracts. By fostering an environment of warmth and kindness, the Gingerbread Golem draws in positive energies, blessings, and goodwill.

- **Attracting Harmony:** The sweet aroma of spices and baked gingerbread fills a home with a sense of peace and unity, creating a haven of magical protection.

- **Welcoming Prosperity:** In many cultures, sweetness is associated with abundance and good fortune. The Golem becomes a magnet for these energies, enhancing its protective and guiding qualities.

Crafting Sweetness with Intention

The magic of the Gingerbread Golem lies in the intention infused during its creation. To harness the Spirit of Sweetness effectively, every step of the process—from mixing the dough to decorating the figure—should be imbued with mindfulness and purpose.

1. Choosing Ingredients with Purpose

Each ingredient in a Gingerbread Golem contributes to its magical essence. Understanding the properties of these ingredients helps you align your intentions with the Golem's purpose.

- **Molasses:** Grounding and stabilizing energy; provides the Golem with resilience.
- **Honey or Sugar:** Sweetness to attract positivity and diffuse negativity.
- **Ginger:** A fiery spice for protection and empowerment.
- **Cinnamon:** Enhances harmony and amplifies the Golem's magical presence.
- **Clove:** A protective spice that seals the Golem's energy.

2. Infusing Energy During Creation

As you prepare your Gingerbread Golem, focus on the intention behind each action.

- **Mixing the Dough:** Visualize the dough absorbing your intentions for protection, guidance, and sweetness.
- **Shaping the Golem:** Consider the form you wish your Golem to take, symbolizing its role in your life.

- **Decorating with Care:** Each embellishment—whether candy buttons or icing sigils—should be placed with purpose, adding layers of meaning and protection.

3. Activating the Spirit of Sweetness

Once your Golem is complete, the final step is to awaken its spirit through a simple yet powerful ritual. (Details of this process are outlined in Chapter 3: Activating Your Golem.)

The Dual Nature of Sweetness

The Spirit of Sweetness is not about vulnerability; it is a strategic strength. The Gingerbread Golem teaches us that protection need not come from aggression but can emerge from a place of kindness and resilience. Sweetness in magic is an act of defiance against negativity, proving that light can triumph without darkness.

By understanding the Spirit of Sweetness, you lay the foundation for a deep and meaningful connection with your Gingerbread Golem. It becomes not only a magical ally but also a reflection of your own ability to blend compassion with strength in the pursuit of a harmonious life.

Let sweetness guide your path and fortify your defenses as you embark on this magical journey with the Gingerbread Golem by your side.

Chapter 2: Building the Gingerbread Golem

Creating a Gingerbread Golem is a sacred act of magical crafting, blending the art of baking with the power of intention. Each ingredient you choose and every step of the process contribute to the Golem's strength as a protector and guide. This chapter provides a step-by-step ritual for crafting your Gingerbread Golem and explains the symbolic meanings behind its ingredients, ensuring your creation is infused with purpose and magic.

Step-by-Step Ritual for Crafting the Gingerbread Golem

This ritual transforms the act of baking into a magical practice. Approach it with focus, mindfulness, and respect for the energies you are summoning.

Preparation: Setting the Magical Space

Before you begin crafting your Gingerbread Golem, prepare your space to ensure it is energetically conducive to magic.

1. **Cleanse Your Kitchen:**
   - Physically clean your workspace to remove clutter and negative energy.
   - Use a smoke cleansing method (e.g., sage, palo santo, or rosemary) or a spray made with salt water to spiritually cleanse the area.
2. **Gather Your Tools and Ingredients:**
   - Arrange all your ingredients and baking tools. Treat them as sacred objects in your ritual.
3. **Set Your Intentions:**
   - Take a moment to focus on why you are creating the Gingerbread Golem. Visualize it as a protector or guide, radiating warmth and strength. Speak your intention aloud if you feel called to do so.
4. **Create an Altar or Focal Point:**
   - Light a candle (brown or gold for grounding and abundance) and place it nearby as you work. You can also in-

clude symbols of the Gingerbread Golem, such as spices, candy, or small protective talismans.

**The Recipe for the Gingerbread Golem
Ingredients (Symbolic Meanings):**

- **2 cups all-purpose flour:** Represents stability and grounding. Flour is the foundation of the Golem's form.
- **1 tsp baking soda:** A catalyst for growth and expansion, allowing the Golem's energy to rise and expand.
- **1 tsp ground cinnamon:** A protective spice that amplifies harmony and wards off negativity.
- **1 tsp ground ginger:** Adds fiery protection and strength, empowering the Golem to stand firm against harm.
- **½ tsp ground cloves:** A spice of sealing and protection, ensuring the Golem's energy remains intact.
- **½ tsp ground nutmeg:** Symbolizes luck and enhances the Golem's ability to attract blessings.
- **½ cup unsalted butter:** Represents softness and nurturing energy, balancing the Golem's strength.
- **½ cup dark brown sugar:** Attracts abundance and binds the energies of sweetness and protection.
- **¼ cup molasses:** Grounding and fortifying energy; molasses connects the Golem to the earth's stability.
- **1 large egg:** A symbol of life and the activation of the Golem's essence.

The Ritual of Crafting

1. **Mixing the Dough:**
   - Combine the flour, baking soda, cinnamon, ginger, cloves, and nutmeg in a bowl.
   - As you mix, say:

"Earth and spice, strength and grace,
By my hands, this Golem I place.
Protection strong, guidance sweet,
A magical guardian, whole and complete."

1. **Creaming Butter and Sugar:**
   - Beat the butter and brown sugar until light and fluffy. Add the molasses and egg, blending them with intention.
   - Visualize warmth and protection infusing the mixture, creating a foundation of care and strength.
2. **Combining the Elements:**
   - Gradually mix the dry ingredients into the wet ingredients to form the dough. Knead it gently, feeling the energy of creation in your hands. Imagine shaping the Golem's essence as you work.
3. **Chilling the Dough:**
   - Wrap the dough and let it chill for 30 minutes to an hour. During this time, meditate on the Golem's purpose. Hold the vision of the finished figure in your mind.

Shaping the Golem

1. **Roll Out the Dough:**
   - Roll the dough on a floured surface, about ¼ inch thick. Focus on the Golem's protective and guiding nature as you handle the dough.
2. **Cut the Golem's Form:**
   - Use a gingerbread man cookie cutter or shape the Golem freehand. If desired, personalize the Golem with symbols, runes, or initials etched into its surface.
3. **Decorate the Golem:**
   - Use candy, icing, or edible decorations to give the Golem character. Each addition should carry intention:
     - **Candy Eyes:** Vision and clarity to watch over your space.
     - **Buttons or Beads:** Symbols of strength and connection.
     - **Icing Sigils:** Magical symbols for protection, guidance, or other attributes.

Baking the Golem

1. **Bake with Intention:**
   - Place the shaped Golem on a baking sheet and bake at 350°F (175°C) for 8–10 minutes. As the Golem bakes, speak your intention aloud:

"Through fire's embrace, strength will grow,
Protector sweet, with power aglow.
Guide my path, defend my space,
A guardian born in this sacred place."

1. **Cooling the Golem:**
   - Allow the Golem to cool completely before handling. Use this time to ground yourself and prepare for the activation ritual (covered in Chapter 3).

The Symbolism of the Ingredients

Every ingredient in the Gingerbread Golem carries a magical property, contributing to its essence:

- **Flour:** Grounding and stability. It provides the physical structure and represents the foundation of the Golem's protective energy.
- **Molasses:** A deep, rich substance tied to the earth's energy. It fortifies the Golem's connection to stability and resilience.
- **Ginger:** A fiery spice that empowers and protects. It lends courage and strength to the Golem.
- **Cinnamon:** Known for its protective and harmonizing qualities, it amplifies the Golem's ability to create a safe, peaceful environment.
- **Clove:** A spice of sealing and banishment, clove ensures the Golem's energy is not easily disrupted.

- **Nutmeg:** Associated with good fortune and abundance, it enhances the Golem's ability to attract positive energy.
- **Butter and Sugar:** Represent nurturing and sweetness, balancing the fiery and protective aspects of the other ingredients.
- **Egg:** A universal symbol of life and vitality, it activates and enlivens the Golem's essence.

Closing the Ritual

Once your Gingerbread Golem is baked, it is ready to be activated (see Chapter 3). Display it in your home or workspace as a magical ally. Each time you see it, remember the intentions you infused into its creation and trust in its protective and guiding energies.

By carefully crafting your Gingerbread Golem with these steps, you create a powerful magical companion that embodies the Spirit of Sweetness, ready to guard your space and guide your path during the festive season.

Chapter 3: Activating Your Golem

The Gingerbread Golem, now crafted and decorated, is a powerful vessel waiting to be infused with life and purpose. This chapter will guide you through the process of activation, breathing magical energy into your creation. By channeling your intentions and focusing your emotional energy, you awaken the Golem's spirit, transforming it from a charming confection into a living magical ally.

The Purpose of Activation

Activation is the process of imbuing your Gingerbread Golem with magical life. It is through this ritual that the Golem becomes a protector, guide, and energetic companion.

- **From Static to Dynamic:** Without activation, the Golem remains a symbolic object. Activation transforms it into a magical being with a purpose.
- **Connection to Spirit:** The ritual connects your Golem to the energies of protection, guidance, and harmony, anchoring it to your intentions.
- **Personalized Power:** By infusing your emotional energy and focus, you ensure the Golem resonates uniquely with your needs.

Preparation for Activation

Before you begin the activation ritual, prepare your space and yourself to ensure the process is focused and sacred.

1. Cleanse the Space

- Use a cleansing method such as smoke (sage, rosemary, or incense) or sound (bells, chimes, or singing bowls) to clear the energy in your workspace.
- Place the Gingerbread Golem in the center of your altar or a clean, flat surface.

2. Gather Ritual Tools

Prepare the following items:

- **A candle** (brown for grounding, gold for empowerment, or white for purity).
- **Incense** (cinnamon, ginger, or clove for protection and activation).
- **A bowl of water** (symbolizing life and fluidity).
- **A small bowl of sugar or honey** (representing sweetness and nurturing energy).
- **A written intention** for the Golem's purpose, if desired.

3. Center Yourself

Take a few deep breaths to center your energy. Visualize yourself surrounded by light, calm, and focus. Set your intention clearly in your mind: What role will the Golem play in your life? Whether it is protection, guidance, or harmony, hold that purpose firmly in your thoughts.

Step-by-Step Activation Ritual
Step 1: Light the Candle

- Light the candle and place it in front of your Golem. Say:

"Fire's light, ignite this space,
By flame and spirit, life embrace.
Protector born of dough and sweet,
Awaken now, your form complete."

Visualize the candle's flame illuminating your Golem, filling it with warmth and energy.

Step 2: Cleanse and Bless

- Take the bowl of water and dip your fingers into it. Sprinkle a few drops onto the Golem while saying:

"Water flows, a sacred stream,
Cleanse this form, fulfill the dream.
By fluid life, its soul ignite,
A guardian strong, both day and night."

- Next, sprinkle a pinch of sugar or honey over the Golem. Say:

"Sweetness bind and love protect,
Your strength grows now, in all respect.
By sugar's charm and honey's grace,
Your magic thrives in this sacred place."

Step 3: Speak Its Purpose

Hold your written intention (if you prepared one) or simply speak aloud the Golem's purpose. Address it directly, as though it is already alive:

- Example: *"Gingerbread Golem, I awaken you as my protector and guide. Stand watch over my home, guard against harm, and bring clarity to my path. In your sweetness, I find harmony; in your strength, I find safety. So it is."*

Speak with conviction, as the power of your voice carries the energy needed to awaken the Golem.

Step 4: Enchant with a Chant

Begin a chant to solidify the activation. Repeat the following lines three times, building your energy with each repetition:

"By spice and sweet, by fire and dough,
A guardian's strength begins to grow.
Protector wise, a guide so true,
Gingerbread Golem, I awaken you!"

As you chant, visualize a glowing light surrounding the Golem, growing brighter with each repetition until it radiates energy.

Step 5: Seal the Energy

To seal the activation, touch the Golem gently with both hands. Close your eyes and visualize your energy flowing into it. Feel gratitude for its presence and purpose. Whisper:

"Awake, protector, guide, and friend,
Your watch begins; your strength will mend.
By sweetness strong and grounded might,
Guard and guide both day and night."

Take a moment of silence to honor the newly awakened spirit within the Golem.

The Role of Intention and Emotional Energy

The success of the activation ritual depends heavily on your intention and emotional energy. These elements serve as the "fuel" for the Golem's magical life.

1. Clear Intention

- Be specific about the Golem's purpose. Vague intentions dilute its energy, while clear, focused intentions enhance its effectiveness.
- Examples of clear intentions:
    - *"Protect my home from harm."*
    - *"Guide me in making wise decisions."*
    - *"Foster peace and harmony within my family."*

2. Emotional Energy

- Your emotions act as a catalyst, charging the Golem with vibrant energy. Feelings of love, gratitude, and excitement are particularly powerful.
- Avoid performing the ritual if you feel anxious or distracted, as negative emotions can interfere with the activation process.

Signs of Activation

Once the activation ritual is complete, you may notice subtle signs that the Gingerbread Golem has awakened. These could include:

- A warm or comforting sensation when near the Golem.
- A sense of calm or protection in its presence.
- Feeling intuitively guided or supported after the ritual.

Caring for Your Golem

After activation, your Golem becomes a magical ally. Treat it with respect and care:

- **Placement:** Place it in a prominent location where it can "watch over" the space it is protecting or guiding.
- **Offerings:** Occasionally place small offerings near the Golem, such as a sprinkle of cinnamon or a drop of honey, to maintain its energy.
- **Gratitude:** Acknowledge its presence regularly. A simple "thank you" helps strengthen your bond.

Conclusion

Activating your Gingerbread Golem is a transformative experience that merges your intentions with magical practice. Through this ritual, you breathe life into your creation, establishing a powerful connection with a protective and guiding force. As your Golem begins its watch, you can take comfort in knowing that it is more than a festive decoration—it is a magical companion, ready to shield, guide, and inspire you throughout the holiday season and beyond.

Chapter 4: The Golem as Protector

The Gingerbread Golem's role as a protector is one of its most powerful and enduring aspects. Its very essence is steeped in magical energies designed to guard your home, family, and spiritual well-being. This chapter explores protective spells you can cast with your Gingerbread Golem and how to create a protective boundary for your home and hearth.

The Protective Nature of the Gingerbread Golem

The Gingerbread Golem's magical protection is rooted in its symbolic strength, sweetness, and connection to the energies of the home. As a magical ally, it acts as both a shield against harm and a barrier that repels negativity. Unlike aggressive forms of protection, the Golem's sweetness diffuses harmful energies, creating an environment of peace and security.

Why the Gingerbread Golem is Effective for Protection

1. **Sweetness as a Barrier:** The sugary components of the Golem create a shield that attracts positivity and deflects negative influences.

2. **Grounding Energy:** The spices and ingredients anchor the Golem's protective energies, ensuring a stable and consistent force.

3. **Symbolic Watchfulness:** The Golem's form represents vigilance, standing as a sentinel for your home.

Protective Spells That Utilize the Golem

Below are several spells that harness the Gingerbread Golem's protective energy. Each spell is designed to address specific forms of protection, from guarding against physical threats to repelling spiritual harm.

1. The Guardian Glow Spell

This spell enhances the Golem's ability to shield your space by imbuing it with radiant protective energy.

What You'll Need:

- Your activated Gingerbread Golem
- A gold or white candle (for protective light)
- A pinch of cinnamon
- A piece of clear quartz (optional)

Instructions:

1. Place the Gingerbread Golem in the center of your altar or a flat surface.
2. Light the candle and sprinkle a pinch of cinnamon around the base of the Golem.
3. Hold the quartz (if using) and visualize a warm golden light surrounding the Golem. Say:

"Guardian sweet, protector strong,
Shield this home from all that's wrong.
Let your glow repel the night,
Keep us safe in your golden light."

1. Let the candle burn for at least 15 minutes while focusing on the Golem absorbing and radiating protective energy.

2. The Spiced Ward Spell

This spell creates an energetic barrier using the Golem's connection to spices associated with protection and banishment.

What You'll Need:

- Ground cloves, cinnamon, and ginger
- A small bowl of salt
- Your Gingerbread Golem

Instructions:

1. Mix the spices and salt in a small bowl.
2. Place the Gingerbread Golem in the area you wish to protect (e.g., near the main entrance of your home).
3. Sprinkle the mixture in a circle around the Golem while chanting:

"Spices bold and salt so pure,
Guard this home, protection sure.
No harm shall enter, none shall stay,
This sacred space is safe each day."

1. Leave the circle undisturbed as a continuous protective ward.

3. The Sweet Shield Spell

This spell uses the sweetness of the Golem to neutralize negativity and foster peace.

What You'll Need:

- A small bowl of honey
- A piece of paper and a pen
- Your Gingerbread Golem

Instructions:

1. Write down any fears, worries, or threats you wish the Golem to protect you from on the piece of paper.
2. Fold the paper and place it beneath the Golem.
3. Dip your finger into the honey and gently touch the Golem's heart or chest area. As you do, say:

"Sweetness binds and love protects,
This Golem shields with no regrets.
Harm dissolved, no ill remains,
Peace and joy shall here sustain."

1. Leave the honey offering near the Golem for a day before disposing of it outdoors.

Creating a Protective Boundary for Home and Hearth

In addition to specific spells, your Gingerbread Golem can be used to create a protective boundary around your home. This boundary acts as a magical barrier that repels negativity and prevents harm from entering your space.

1. The Hearth Circle

The hearth is the symbolic and energetic heart of the home. Use your Gingerbread Golem to anchor protective energy at this central point.

Instructions:

1. Place your Gingerbread Golem near your fireplace, kitchen stove, or a central location in your home.
2. Sprinkle a mix of salt and cinnamon around the area in a circle, focusing on creating a barrier that extends throughout your home.
3. Light a white candle and say:

"Hearth and home, a sacred flame,
Protection strong in this Golem's name.
Boundaries set, no harm shall stay,
This home is safe, both night and day."

1. Let the candle burn safely for at least 10 minutes to reinforce the boundary.

2. The Doorway Ward

Protecting the main entrance to your home is essential for keeping out unwanted energies. The Gingerbread Golem can serve as a sentinel for your doorway.

Instructions:

1. Place the Gingerbread Golem near your main entrance, facing outward as though watching over the space.
2. Hang a cinnamon stick or protective sigil above the door to amplify the effect.
3. Sprinkle a small line of salt across the threshold while saying:

"At this door, no ill shall pass,
Harm dissolves like shattered glass.
Golem strong, stand firm and true,
Protect this home in all I do."

1. Reapply the salt barrier monthly or after heavy foot traffic.

3. The Perimeter Shield

For comprehensive protection, extend the Golem's energy to the boundaries of your property.

Instructions:

1. Walk the perimeter of your property with the Gingerbread Golem in hand.
2. As you walk, sprinkle a mix of salt and cinnamon, imagining a protective dome forming over your entire home.
3. At each corner of the property, stop and say:

"Golem of sweetness, guardian of might,
Shield this space with your golden light.

Protect this land, its borders hold,
A sacred space, both strong and bold."

1. Once the perimeter is complete, return the Golem to its designated spot indoors.

Strengthening Your Golem's Protective Energy

Over time, you may feel the need to recharge or strengthen your Golem's protective energy. Here are a few ways to maintain its potency:

- **Regular Offerings:** Place small offerings, such as a sprinkle of sugar or a drop of honey, near the Golem to renew its energy.
- **Seasonal Cleansing:** Cleanse the Golem's space with incense or a sound bowl to remove accumulated negativity.
- **Daily Acknowledgment:** Speak a simple gratitude phrase, such as *"Thank you for your protection,"* to keep the connection alive.

Conclusion

The Gingerbread Golem, as a protector, is a powerful ally in guarding your home and hearth. By casting protective spells and creating boundaries with its energy, you can transform your living space into a sanctuary of peace and safety. With its sweetness and strength working in harmony, the Golem not only shields against harm but also fosters an environment of warmth and positivity, ensuring your home is a sacred haven during the festive season and beyond.

Chapter 5: The Golem as Guide

Beyond its role as a protector, the Gingerbread Golem serves as a spiritual guide, offering clarity and wisdom during the holiday season's often chaotic energy. Working with the Golem for divination allows you to tap into its magical essence to receive insights, resolve uncertainties, and find your path amidst the festivities. This chapter explores how to harness the Gingerbread Golem's guiding energy through divination tools and rituals designed to align your intentions with the magic of the season.

The Golem's Guiding Nature

The Gingerbread Golem's essence is infused with warmth, intuition, and a deep connection to the energies of harmony and clarity. As a guide, the Golem:

- **Enhances Intuition:** Its symbolic sweetness helps dissolve mental blocks and fosters intuitive clarity.
- **Facilitates Communication:** By acting as an energetic intermediary, the Golem can help you connect with your higher self, spirit guides, or seasonal energies.
- **Provides Direction:** Its steady presence grounds you, making it easier to identify solutions to challenges or find guidance when feeling lost.

Preparing the Gingerbread Golem for Guidance

Before using the Golem as a divination tool or guide, ensure it is properly activated (see Chapter 3). Additionally, you'll want to prepare your space and mindset for this sacred work.

1. Cleanse and Recharge the Golem

If you've been using the Golem as a protector, cleanse its energy before engaging it as a guide. This can be done with incense, sound, or light:

- Burn cinnamon or rosemary incense and pass the Golem through the smoke.
- Ring a bell or chime near the Golem to refresh its energy.
- Place the Golem near a lit white candle for a few minutes to infuse it with clarity.

2. Set Your Intention

Clearly define the type of guidance you seek. The more specific your intention, the more focused the Golem's responses will be. For example:

- *"What is the best path forward for my career in the new year?"*
- *"How can I resolve this family conflict?"*
- *"What lessons do I need to learn this holiday season?"*

3. Gather Divination Tools

The Gingerbread Golem can work in conjunction with traditional divination tools or serve as a standalone guide. Consider having the following items nearby:

- Tarot or oracle cards
- A pendulum
- A scrying bowl or mirror

• A notebook or journal to record insights

Working with the Golem for Divination

The following techniques incorporate the Gingerbread Golem into divination practices, allowing its magical energy to guide your intuition.

1. The Golem Oracle Ritual

This simple ritual uses the Golem as a focus for receiving messages and insights.

What You'll Need:

• Your Gingerbread Golem
• A candle (white or gold for clarity)
• A pen and paper or a journal

Instructions:

1. Place the Golem on your altar or workspace.
2. Light the candle and focus on the flame for a moment, allowing your mind to quiet.
3. Speak your intention aloud:

"Guardian sweet, guide so wise,
Help me see with clear eyes.
Show me paths both near and far,
Illuminate my guiding star."

1. Close your eyes and place your hands gently on the Golem. Pay attention to any images, words, or feelings that arise. These are your messages.
2. Record your impressions in your journal. If anything is unclear, ask follow-up questions and repeat the process.

2. The Sweet Pendulum Reading

The Golem can act as an anchor for pendulum divination, enhancing clarity and grounding your responses.

What You'll Need:

- A pendulum
- Your Gingerbread Golem
- A small plate or placemat for the Golem to "stand guard"

Instructions:

1. Set up the Golem in front of you, placing it on a flat surface where it can "watch" over the pendulum.
2. Hold your pendulum steady and focus on the Golem, silently asking it to guide the pendulum's movements.
3. Begin with simple yes/no questions to establish the pendulum's directional patterns (e.g., "Show me yes" and "Show me no").
4. Ask your questions, trusting the Golem to guide the pendulum's answers. For example:
    - *"Is this decision in my highest good?"*
    - *"Should I pursue this opportunity now?"*
5. Thank the Golem when finished and place the pendulum near it to "rest."

3. Gingerbread Tarot Spread

This tarot spread incorporates the Golem's guiding energy to provide insights for the holiday season or a specific situation.

What You'll Need:

- A tarot or oracle deck
- Your Gingerbread Golem

The Spread:

- **Card 1 (Past):** What lessons have I carried into this moment?
- **Card 2 (Present):** What energies are surrounding me now?
- **Card 3 (Guidance):** What message does the Golem have for me?
- **Card 4 (Future):** Where will this path lead?

Instructions:

1. Shuffle the deck while focusing on your question or intention.
2. Place the Golem at the head of your spread as a symbolic "guide."
3. Draw and lay out the cards according to the positions listed above.
4. Interpret the cards with the Golem's protective and guiding energy in mind. Use its symbolism as inspiration for understanding the messages.

Rituals for Receiving Guidance During the Holiday Season

The holiday season is a time of heightened energy, both joyful and stressful. Use the following rituals to align yourself with the Golem's guiding wisdom during this unique time of year.

1. The Festive Path Ritual

This ritual is ideal for when you're faced with a major decision or feel uncertain about the best path forward.

What You'll Need:

- Your Gingerbread Golem
- A white or gold candle
- A small dish of cinnamon

Instructions:

1. Light the candle and place the dish of cinnamon near the Golem.
2. Sit quietly, holding the Golem in your hands or placing it in front of you.
3. Say:

"Gingerbread guide, with sweetness and might,
Illuminate my path in the holiday light.
Show me the way, steady and true,
Guide my steps in all I do."

1. Focus on your question or decision. Close your eyes and visualize the candlelight expanding into a pathway. Pay attention to any symbols, colors, or feelings that emerge.
2. When finished, sprinkle a pinch of cinnamon around the Golem as a token of gratitude.

2. The Holiday Insight Ritual

This ritual helps you gain clarity about the lessons or blessings of the holiday season.

What You'll Need:

- Your Gingerbread Golem
- A journal or notebook
- A cup of herbal tea (cinnamon, ginger, or peppermint)

Instructions:

1. Prepare your space with calming music or candles to create a reflective atmosphere.
2. Sit with your Golem and tea. Take a few deep breaths to center yourself.
3. Ask the Golem: *"What wisdom does this season hold for me?"*
4. Sip the tea slowly, allowing any thoughts, images, or emotions to surface.
5. Write down your reflections in your journal, trusting the Golem to guide your awareness.

Maintaining the Golem's Guiding Energy

To keep your Gingerbread Golem aligned with its guiding role:

- **Refresh Its Energy:** Regularly cleanse and recharge the Golem, especially after intense divination sessions.
- **Acknowledge Its Guidance:** Offer a small token of thanks, such as a sprinkle of sugar or a spoken word of gratitude.
- **Reflect Often:** Keep a journal of the insights you receive through the Golem to track patterns or recurring messages.

Conclusion

The Gingerbread Golem's guiding energy is a powerful tool for navigating the complexities of the holiday season and beyond. By working with it through divination and ritual, you can access its sweetness, clarity, and wisdom, finding answers and direction when you need them most. Let the Golem be your trusted guide, lighting the way through both festive joy and life's uncertainties.

Part II: Sweet Spells and Festive Rituals

Chapter 6: The Sugar Shield Spell

The **Sugar Shield Spell** is a simple yet powerful defensive technique that uses sugar and spices to create an energetic barrier against negativity. Sweetness is often underestimated in magical work, but its ability to diffuse harm and foster harmony makes it an exceptional tool for protection. This chapter provides a detailed guide to casting the Sugar Shield Spell, explaining the symbolic significance of each ingredient and the steps to create a ward that safeguards your space.

The Magic of Sweetness and Spice

The Sugar Shield Spell combines the sweetness of sugar with the fiery and protective properties of spices. Together, they form a magical force that is both nurturing and formidable. Here's why these ingredients are particularly effective:

1. Sugar: The Sweet Diffuser

- Sugar attracts positive energy, dissolving negativity and replacing it with warmth and kindness.
- Its crystalline structure symbolizes clarity and stability, forming a protective layer that is hard to penetrate.

2. Spices: The Fiery Defenders

- **Cinnamon:** A harmonizer and protector, cinnamon creates a warm, energetic shield against harm.
- **Cloves:** Known for their sealing and banishing properties, cloves repel negative entities and intentions.
- **Ginger:** A fiery root that empowers and protects, ginger is ideal for strengthening the spell's defensive properties.
- **Nutmeg:** A spice of luck and abundance, nutmeg enhances the shield's ability to attract positive outcomes.

By combining these elements, the Sugar Shield Spell creates a defensive layer that is both firm and inviting, deterring harm while fostering peace.

When to Use the Sugar Shield Spell

This spell is versatile and can be used in a variety of situations, including:

- **Protecting Your Home:** Create a barrier around your space to keep negativity at bay.
- **Personal Protection:** Use the spell to shield your energy from harmful influences in social or professional settings.
- **Seasonal Safeguards:** Cast the spell during the holiday season to ward off stress, conflicts, or other disruptive energies.

Ingredients and Tools

To cast the Sugar Shield Spell, you'll need the following:

Ingredients

- 1 cup of granulated sugar (or brown sugar for grounding energy)
- 1 teaspoon ground cinnamon
- 1 teaspoon ground ginger
- ½ teaspoon ground cloves
- ½ teaspoon ground nutmeg
- A pinch of salt (for purification and added protection)

Tools

- A small bowl for mixing
- A clean jar or container to store the mixture
- A white or gold candle (optional, for added energy)
- A spoon for sprinkling

Step-by-Step Guide to Casting the Sugar Shield Spell
1. Prepare Your Space

- Choose a quiet, clean area to perform the spell. Clear any clutter and cleanse the space with your preferred method, such as burning incense, ringing a bell, or visualizing white light filling the room.
- Light a white or gold candle to symbolize protection and clarity.

2. Mix the Ingredients

1. In the small bowl, combine the sugar, cinnamon, ginger, cloves, nutmeg, and salt.
2. As you add each ingredient, focus on its protective properties. Speak aloud or silently affirm its purpose:
   - *"Sugar, sweet and clear, dissolve all harm and bring good cheer."*
   - *"Cinnamon, with your fiery might, protect this space both day and night."*
   - *"Cloves, strong and true, banish what seeks to undo."*
   - *"Ginger, fierce and bold, guard this place as I have told."*
   - *"Nutmeg, bring luck and light, shield us in your golden sight."*
   - *"Salt, pure and bright, seal this spell with sacred might."*
3. Mix the ingredients thoroughly while visualizing a shimmering, golden shield forming around you or the space you wish to protect.

3. Charge the Mixture

- Place your hands over the bowl and close your eyes. Focus your energy on the intention of the spell: protection, peace, and positivity.
- Recite the following incantation three times:

"Sweetness strong, a shield I weave,
To guard this place from those who deceive.
Spices bold and salt so pure,
Let no harm cross this threshold's door."

- Imagine the mixture glowing with a soft, golden light, infused with your intention.

4. Apply the Sugar Shield

- To protect a space, sprinkle the mixture lightly around the perimeter of your home, focusing on doorways, windows, and other points of entry. As you sprinkle, say:

"With sugar and spice, I ward this place,
No harm may enter, no ill can trace.
This shield I cast, strong and sweet,
A sacred guard, whole and complete."

- For personal protection, you can carry a small jar of the mixture in your bag or pocket, or sprinkle a tiny amount into your shoes or coat pockets.

Strengthening the Sugar Shield

The Sugar Shield Spell is effective on its own, but you can amplify its power with these techniques:

1. Reinforce with Visualization

Regularly visualize the shield glowing brightly around your home or body. This mental practice helps maintain the spell's energy.

2. Add Seasonal Elements

For holiday-specific protection, incorporate seasonal decorations into your shield. For example:

- Place the Sugar Shield mixture in small decorative jars and display them near entrances.
- Add a sprig of evergreen or a candy cane to the jar for an extra layer of seasonal charm and magic.

3. Recharge the Shield

Over time, the shield's energy may weaken. Recharge it by repeating the incantation while holding the mixture or sprinkling a fresh batch around your space.

Practical Tips for Success

- **Dispose of Old Mixture Properly:** When you feel the mixture has absorbed negativity, dispose of it outdoors, such as sprinkling it in your garden or burying it in the earth.
- **Be Mindful of Pets:** If you have pets, ensure the sprinkled mixture is placed in areas they cannot access, as some spices may not be safe for animals.
- **Combine with Other Protections:** The Sugar Shield works well alongside physical wards, such as protective crystals or charms placed at entry points.

Conclusion

The Sugar Shield Spell is a powerful and accessible way to ward off negativity using the gentle yet potent magic of sweetness and spice. Whether you're protecting your home, yourself, or loved ones, this spell creates a harmonious and nurturing barrier that keeps harmful energies at bay while inviting positivity and joy. By casting the Sugar Shield, you embody the Gingerbread Golem's essence as both protector and guide, ensuring that your space remains a sanctuary of safety and light.

Chapter 7: The Cinnamon of Clarity Ritual

The **Cinnamon of Clarity Ritual** is a powerful cleansing practice designed to clear mental fog, sharpen focus, and invite clear thinking into your life. Cinnamon, with its fiery and invigorating properties, is the key ingredient in this ritual. Known for its ability to enhance mental clarity, improve concentration, and stimulate the senses, cinnamon acts as the catalyst for unlocking your mind's full potential.

This chapter provides a detailed, step-by-step guide to performing the Cinnamon of Clarity Ritual, explaining the symbolism of its ingredients, the ideal times to perform it, and how to incorporate this practice into your magical routine for ongoing mental and spiritual clarity.

The Magic of Cinnamon

Cinnamon is revered in magical traditions for its warming, uplifting, and energizing properties. As a spice, it has been used for centuries in spells and rituals to:

- **Enhance Focus:** Its invigorating scent stimulates the mind and improves mental alertness.
- **Dispel Negativity:** Cinnamon's fiery energy burns away mental fog and confusion, replacing it with clarity.
- **Invite Success:** Often associated with prosperity and success, cinnamon aligns your mind with productive, positive energy.

In the Cinnamon of Clarity Ritual, this spice becomes a magical tool for creating a mental reset, making it particularly useful during times of stress, indecision, or mental fatigue.

When to Perform the Ritual

The Cinnamon of Clarity Ritual is versatile and can be performed whenever you feel mentally clouded or need a boost in focus. However, certain times may enhance its effectiveness:

- **Morning Ritual:** Start your day with clarity and purpose by performing this ritual in the morning.
- **Before a Major Decision:** Use it to gain insight and mental clarity when faced with important choices.
- **During the New Moon:** Align with the energy of new beginnings and clear your mind for fresh ideas.
- **Before Meditation or Study:** Prepare your mind for deep focus or learning.

Ingredients and Tools

To perform the Cinnamon of Clarity Ritual, gather the following:

Ingredients

- 1 cinnamon stick (or 1 teaspoon ground cinnamon)
- 1 tablespoon dried rosemary (for cleansing and mental focus)
- 1 teaspoon dried peppermint or fresh mint leaves (for mental refreshment)
- 1 tablespoon sea salt (to purify and ground energy)
- 1 lemon (sliced, for its clarifying and uplifting energy)

Tools

- A bowl of warm water
- A small white or gold candle (to symbolize clarity and focus)
- A small cloth or towel (optional, for grounding touch)
- A clean space to sit and focus

Step-by-Step Cinnamon of Clarity Ritual
1. Prepare Your Space

- Begin by cleansing the area where you'll perform the ritual. Use your preferred method, such as burning rosemary, ringing a bell, or visualizing white light filling the space.
- Place your tools and ingredients on a clean surface, arranging them thoughtfully to create an inviting and sacred environment.

2. Light the Candle

- Light the white or gold candle and set it near the bowl of warm water. The candle's flame symbolizes clarity and the illumination of the mind. Say:

"By fire's light, my path is clear,
Mental fog shall disappear.
Focus bright, I call to me,
Clarity now, so mote it be."

3. Create the Cleansing Mixture

- Add the cinnamon stick (or ground cinnamon), dried rosemary, dried peppermint, and sea salt to the bowl of warm water.
- Squeeze the juice of the lemon slices into the water, then drop the slices into the bowl.
- Stir the mixture clockwise with your hand or a spoon, visualizing the ingredients blending their energies to create a potion of clarity and focus.

4. Cleanse Your Hands

- Dip your hands into the bowl and gently cleanse them with the mixture. As you do, imagine the water washing away mental fog and distractions. Say:

"With cinnamon's fire and rosemary's might,
I cleanse my mind and restore my sight.
Peppermint fresh, salt so pure,
Mental clarity shall endure."

5. Perform a Focused Visualization

- Close your eyes and hold the cinnamon stick (or, if using ground cinnamon, touch the bowl's rim). Envision a golden light surrounding your head, penetrating your mind, and dissolving any lingering confusion.
- Visualize your thoughts organizing themselves like pieces of a puzzle coming together, leaving you with a sense of calm and focus.

6. Conclude the Ritual

- Dip the cloth or towel into the bowl and gently press it to your forehead or the back of your neck. Feel the cooling, refreshing energy spreading through your body.
- Extinguish the candle and say:

"This work is done; my mind is clear,
I walk my path without fear.
Focus strong, my thoughts aligned,
Peace and clarity fill my mind."

Practical Applications of the Ritual

The Cinnamon of Clarity Ritual can be adapted or repeated as needed. Here are a few ways to integrate it into your daily or magical practice:

- **Morning Focus Boost:** Keep a jar of the cleansing mixture in the fridge and use it in the morning to refresh your hands and face for a quick clarity boost.
- **Pre-Meditation Ritual:** Perform the ritual before meditating to deepen your mental focus and connection.
- **Decision-Making Support:** Use the ritual when journaling or brainstorming solutions to help organize your thoughts.

Strengthening the Ritual's Energy

For additional potency, consider these enhancements:

- **Use Affirmations:** While performing the ritual, repeat affirmations such as:
    - *"My mind is clear and focused."*
    - *"I release confusion and embrace clarity."*
- **Pair with Crystals:** Place clear quartz, citrine, or fluorite near your workspace to enhance focus and mental clarity.
- **Incorporate Essential Oils:** Add a drop of cinnamon or rosemary essential oil to the bowl of water for added aromatic power.

The Symbolism of the Ingredients

Each ingredient in the ritual plays a unique role in clearing mental fog and inviting focus:

- **Cinnamon:** Provides fiery energy to burn away mental clutter and spark clarity.
- **Rosemary:** Enhances memory and mental focus, while purifying the mind.
- **Peppermint:** Refreshes the senses, clearing away mental fatigue.
- **Sea Salt:** Grounds energy, purifies thoughts, and removes distractions.
- **Lemon:** Uplifts and energizes, brightening both mood and mental processes.

Signs the Ritual is Working

You may notice several signs that the Cinnamon of Clarity Ritual has been effective:

- A sense of lightness or mental relief.
- Increased focus and productivity.
- Greater ease in making decisions or organizing thoughts.
- Feeling refreshed and energized.

Conclusion

The Cinnamon of Clarity Ritual is a simple yet profoundly effective way to dispel mental fog and invite focus into your life. By working with the magical properties of cinnamon, rosemary, and other cleansing ingredients, this ritual aligns your mind with clarity and purpose. Whether used as a daily practice or a special remedy for moments of overwhelm, the Cinnamon of Clarity Ritual empowers you to navigate life with a clear and focused mind.

Chapter 8: The Molasses Binding

Binding spells are a cornerstone of protective magic, offering a way to restrict and neutralize harmful influences without causing harm. **The Molasses Binding Spell** is a unique approach that uses the slow, sticky properties of molasses to metaphorically "bind" negativity, toxic influences, or harmful individuals, ensuring they cannot disrupt your life or energy. This spell works through the principle of sympathetic magic, where molasses' properties reflect the desired magical outcome.

This chapter provides a step-by-step guide to performing the Molasses Binding Spell, including its purpose, symbolic elements, detailed instructions, and tips for maintaining its protective energy.

The Purpose of the Molasses Binding Spell

The Molasses Binding Spell is ideal for situations where you need to neutralize or restrain a harmful influence. This could include:

- **Toxic Relationships:** Preventing the negative impact of a person's energy without wishing them harm.
- **Persistent Negativity:** Blocking recurring negative patterns or energy from your environment.
- **External Harm:** Stopping the effects of malicious intentions, such as gossip, envy, or hostility.

Unlike aggressive counter-spells, binding magic focuses on neutralizing the source of harm rather than returning it to its sender. This aligns with ethical magical practices that prioritize harm reduction and maintaining balance.

The Symbolism of Molasses

Molasses plays a central role in this spell due to its unique properties and symbolic significance:

- **Stickiness:** Represents the ability to trap and hold harmful energy, preventing it from spreading.
- **Dark Color:** Symbolizes grounding and absorbing negativity.
- **Slow Movement:** Reflects the intention to restrict and slow down harmful actions or influences.
- **Sweetness:** Balances the binding energy with compassion, ensuring the spell does not cause unnecessary harm.

By incorporating molasses into this binding spell, you create a magical tool that is both effective and aligned with ethical intentions.

Ingredients and Tools

To perform the Molasses Binding Spell, you will need the following:

Ingredients

- 1 jar of molasses
- A small piece of paper
- A black or dark blue pen (for protection and banishment energy)
- A pinch of salt (for purification and grounding)
- A pinch of cayenne pepper (optional, for added potency in stopping harm)
- A small black candle (or white as a universal substitute)

Tools

- A fireproof bowl or cauldron
- A spoon (to stir the molasses)
- A quiet, clean space to work

Step-by-Step Guide to the Molasses Binding Spell
1. Prepare Your Space

1. Choose a quiet location where you can perform the spell undisturbed.
2. Cleanse the space using your preferred method, such as burning sage, palo santo, or rosemary, or by visualizing white light filling the area.
3. Arrange your tools and ingredients on a clean surface. Place the candle in the center of your workspace.

2. Set Your Intention

- Take a moment to focus on the purpose of the spell. Clearly define what you wish to bind, whether it's a harmful influence, toxic behavior, or negative energy.
- Write the name of the person, behavior, or situation you wish to bind on the piece of paper. If you are binding a person, be specific but remain ethical—focus on restricting their harmful actions, not causing harm to them.

Example:

- *"I bind [name] from causing harm to me or others."*
- *"I bind this toxic pattern of self-doubt and negativity."*

3. Activate the Molasses

1. Open the jar of molasses and hold it in your hands.
2. Visualize the molasses absorbing all harmful energy and intentions, becoming a sticky trap for negativity. Say:

"Molasses dark, so thick and slow,
Trap the harm that seeks to grow.
By your power, I bind this force,
To do no harm, to change its course."

1. Sprinkle the salt and cayenne pepper into the molasses and stir it clockwise (to neutralize energy and protect) while focusing on your intention.

4. Bind the Paper

1. Roll or fold the piece of paper tightly, focusing on the harmful influence being contained and neutralized.
2. Dip the paper into the molasses, ensuring it is completely coated. As you do, chant:

"Sticky and strong, you hold it tight,
Bound in darkness, removed from sight.
No harm shall come, no ill shall flow,
This binding holds; let peace now grow."

1. Place the coated paper in the fireproof bowl or cauldron.

5. Seal the Spell

1. Light the black or white candle and hold it over the bowl. Allow a few drops of wax to fall onto the molasses-coated paper, sealing the binding.
2. Say:

"With fire's seal, this work is done,
Harm is stopped; the spell has spun.

Bound you are, and bound you'll stay,
Until I choose to take away."

1. Allow the candle to burn down safely or extinguish it if time is limited.

6. Dispose of the Binding

- Once the spell is complete, dispose of the molasses-coated paper in a way that feels final and symbolic. Options include:
    - Burying it in the ground to ground the energy and neutralize it.
    - Placing it in a trash bin far from your home to discard the negativity.
    - Sealing it in a jar and storing it in a hidden place if you wish to maintain the binding indefinitely.

Tips for Success
1. Focus on Ethical Intentions

- Ensure your intention is to prevent harm, not to cause harm. Binding magic is most effective when aligned with balance and fairness.

2. Choose the Right Time

- Perform the spell during the **waning moon** (a phase ideal for banishing and reducing) for maximum potency.

3. Strengthen with Visualization

- Visualize the harmful energy being trapped in the molasses, unable to escape. Imagine it dissolving or shrinking over time.

4. Follow Up with Cleansing

- After performing the spell, cleanse your space and yourself to ensure no residual negative energy lingers.

Signs the Binding is Working

You may notice several signs that the Molasses Binding Spell has taken effect:

- The harmful influence feels less prominent or impactful in your life.
- You experience a sense of relief or peace regarding the situation.
- Communication or actions from the bound person become less frequent or intense.

Maintaining the Binding

Bindings can weaken over time, especially if the energy or situation persists. To maintain the binding:

- Repeat the spell as needed, particularly during the waning moon.
- Recharge the binding by visualizing the molasses holding the harmful energy whenever you think about the situation.

Conclusion

The Molasses Binding Spell is a gentle yet powerful way to neutralize harmful influences and regain control over your life. By using the symbolic properties of molasses and aligning your intention with ethical magic, you create a protective barrier that prevents negativity from disrupting your energy or space. Whether used for personal protection or to manage toxic dynamics, this spell empowers you to take action with compassion and strength.

Chapter 9: Candy Cane Harmony Spell

The holiday season is a time for togetherness, but it can also bring stress, conflicts, and miscommunication. The **Candy Cane Harmony Spell** is a magical ritual designed to foster peace, unity, and goodwill among individuals or within a group. By incorporating the symbolic energy of peppermint and the sweet charm of candy canes, this spell uses the vibrant and refreshing qualities of the season to dissolve discord and promote harmony.

This chapter provides an extensive guide to performing the Candy Cane Harmony Spell, covering its symbolism, step-by-step instructions, and ways to customize it for specific situations.

The Symbolism of Candy Canes and Peppermint

Candy canes, with their iconic red and white stripes and refreshing peppermint flavor, carry powerful magical symbolism:

- **Peppermint:** Known for its invigorating and uplifting properties, peppermint clears emotional and energetic blockages, encourages open communication, and refreshes relationships.
- **Red and White Stripes:** The colors symbolize passion and purity, creating a balance between strong emotions and calm resolution.
- **Sweetness:** The sweetness of the candy cane fosters warmth, kindness, and unity, making it a perfect ingredient for spells focused on harmony.

Purpose of the Candy Cane Harmony Spell

The Candy Cane Harmony Spell is versatile and can be used in various situations to:

- Heal conflicts in relationships or groups.
- Create a harmonious atmosphere during gatherings or family events.
- Encourage open communication and mutual understanding.
- Foster a sense of peace and unity in your home or workplace.

Ingredients and Tools

To cast the Candy Cane Harmony Spell, gather the following:

Ingredients

- 3 candy canes (whole or crushed)
- 1 teaspoon dried peppermint leaves (or a few drops of peppermint essential oil)
- 1 teaspoon honey (for sweetness and unity)
- 1 small pinch of sugar (to enhance positive energy)
- 1 small pinch of cinnamon (to amplify the spell's power)

Tools

- A red or white candle (or both for balance)
- A heatproof bowl or cauldron
- A clean piece of paper and a pen
- A small decorative pouch or jar (optional, for keeping the spell's energy)

Step-by-Step Guide to the Candy Cane Harmony Spell
1. Prepare Your Space

- Choose a calm, clean space where you can focus without interruptions. Cleanse the area using your preferred method, such as burning sage or rosemary, sprinkling salt water, or visualizing white light filling the room.
- Arrange your tools and ingredients on a clean surface. Place the candle at the center of your workspace.

2. Set Your Intention

- Take a few moments to think about the purpose of the spell. What specific harmony do you wish to create?
  - For example: *"I wish to heal the tension in my family"* or *"May peace and unity fill this home."*
- Write your intention clearly on the piece of paper. Fold it and place it beneath the heatproof bowl.

3. Create the Harmony Blend

1. Crush the candy canes into small pieces and place them in the heatproof bowl.
2. Add the dried peppermint leaves (or a few drops of peppermint essential oil), honey, sugar, and cinnamon.
3. As you combine these ingredients, say:

"Sweetness and spice, peppermint clear,
Dissolve all discord, bring us near.
Red and white, pure harmony,
Peace and unity come to me."

1. Stir the mixture clockwise while visualizing a glowing, peaceful energy filling the bowl.

4. Light the Candle

- Light the red or white candle and place it next to the bowl. Focus on the flame as a symbol of resolution and unity. Say:

"Flame so bright, burn steady and strong,
Heal all wounds and right the wrong.
With peppermint pure and candy sweet,
Let harmony reign where hearts now meet."

5. Charge the Mixture

- Hold your hands over the bowl, close your eyes, and imagine the mixture glowing with harmonious energy. Visualize peace spreading like ripples from the bowl, reaching the individuals or space you wish to affect.
- Repeat the following incantation three times:

"By candy sweet and peppermint pure,
Let love and peace now endure.
Discord ends, goodwill remains,
Harmony flows through life's veins."

6. Use the Harmony Blend

- Sprinkle a small amount of the blend around your space, focusing on areas where tension is most likely to arise (e.g., near doorways, gathering spaces, or personal altars).
- If working for a specific group or relationship, create a small pouch or jar with the blend to carry or keep in the area where the group meets.

- For added effect, offer candy canes or peppermint tea to the people involved, imbuing the physical act of sharing with your intention for harmony.

Alternative Applications

The Candy Cane Harmony Spell can be adapted for various situations:

- **Personal Harmony:** If the disharmony is within yourself, use the blend in a bath or sprinkle it in your workspace to create inner peace.
- **Group Events:** Place the mixture in a decorative jar as a centerpiece for gatherings, silently charging it with harmonious energy for all attendees.
- **Gift of Harmony:** Package the blend in small bags or jars and give them as gifts, blessing each one with the intention of spreading peace and unity.

Strengthening the Spell's Energy

- **Daily Affirmations:** Reinforce the spell's energy by speaking affirmations such as:
    - *"Harmony flows through my life effortlessly."*
    - *"Our relationships are filled with understanding and peace."*
- **Visualize Success:** Spend a few minutes each day imagining the people or spaces affected by the spell surrounded by warmth and light.
- **Renew the Spell:** Refresh the energy by lighting the candle and stirring the remaining blend while repeating the incantation.

The Symbolism of the Ingredients

Each ingredient in the Candy Cane Harmony Spell has a specific magical purpose:

- **Candy Canes:** Represent sweetness and unity, dissolving tension and fostering connection.
- **Peppermint:** Clears emotional and energetic blockages, refreshing the mind and spirit.
- **Honey:** Sweetens relationships and promotes cooperation.
- **Sugar:** Attracts positivity and amplifies the spell's effectiveness.
- **Cinnamon:** Adds power to the spell, creating warmth and connection.

Signs of Success

You may notice the following signs that the Candy Cane Harmony Spell is working:

- A noticeable improvement in the mood and energy of the people involved.
- Tensions resolving naturally or communication becoming more open and empathetic.
- A sense of peace and ease in the environment.

Conclusion

The Candy Cane Harmony Spell is a delightful and effective way to dissolve tension and foster peace, whether in relationships, groups, or spaces. By channeling the magical properties of peppermint and candy canes, this spell aligns your intentions with the season's natural energies of love and unity. Whether used during the holidays or throughout the year, the Candy Cane Harmony Spell is a powerful tool for creating an atmosphere of goodwill and togetherness.

Chapter 10: Festive Fortune Cookies

Fortune cookies are not just delightful treats; they can also serve as magical tools for delivering guidance, blessings, or insights. In this chapter, we explore how to craft **Festive Fortune Cookies** imbued with enchantments, transforming them into vessels of wisdom and joy. Whether shared at gatherings or used for personal divination, these enchanted cookies combine the power of intention, magic, and culinary creativity to reveal meaningful fortunes and guidance.

The Magic of Fortune Cookies

Fortune cookies symbolize surprise, serendipity, and the uncovering of hidden wisdom. By enchanting them with intention, they become tools for:

- **Divination:** Offering guidance or answers to specific questions.
- **Blessings:** Delivering good wishes or positive energy to the recipient.
- **Manifestation:** Embedding intentions that align with desired outcomes.

The festive twist comes from incorporating seasonal elements—such as cinnamon, nutmeg, or peppermint—and tailoring the fortunes to align with holiday themes of gratitude, joy, and togetherness.

Ingredients and Tools

To craft enchanted Festive Fortune Cookies, gather the following:

Ingredients

- **For the cookies:**
  - 3 large egg whites
  - ¾ cup granulated sugar
  - ½ cup unsalted butter, melted and cooled
  - ½ cup all-purpose flour
  - 1 teaspoon vanilla extract

  - ○ 1 teaspoon peppermint extract (optional, for a festive twist)
  - ○ A pinch of salt
  - ○ A pinch of cinnamon or nutmeg (optional, for added holiday magic)
- **For the fortunes:**
  - ○ Strips of paper (2-3 inches long and ½ inch wide)
  - ○ A pen or marker for writing fortunes

Tools

- A large mixing bowl
- A baking sheet lined with parchment paper
- A small spoon for spreading the batter
- A small cup or bowl (for shaping the cookies)
- Clean hands and a calm, focused mind for imbuing magical energy

Step-by-Step Guide to Crafting Festive Fortune Cookies
1. Prepare Your Workspace

- Choose a quiet, clean space to work. Set the mood by lighting a white or gold candle to symbolize clarity and joy.
- Cleanse the area using your preferred method, such as burning sage or ringing a bell.
- Arrange all tools and ingredients neatly, and focus your intention on crafting magical cookies that deliver meaningful guidance or blessings.

2. Write the Fortunes

1. On each strip of paper, write a short fortune, blessing, or piece of guidance. Tailor the messages to the holiday season or the purpose of your cookies. Examples include:
   - *"A joyful surprise awaits you this season."*
   - *"Trust in the warmth of your heart to guide you."*
   - *"Harmony and love will fill your home."*
   - *"The path to your wish is clear—walk with faith."*
2. Keep the fortunes positive and uplifting, focusing on themes of joy, clarity, and gratitude.

3. Prepare the Cookie Batter

1. In a large mixing bowl, whisk the egg whites and sugar until the mixture is smooth and slightly frothy.
2. Add the melted butter, vanilla extract, and peppermint extract (if using), and whisk until combined.
3. Sift in the flour, salt, and cinnamon or nutmeg (if using). Gently fold the dry ingredients into the wet mixture until a smooth batter forms.

4. Enchant the Batter

1. Place your hands over the mixing bowl and close your eyes. Visualize golden light flowing from your hands into the batter, imbuing it with your intention.
2. Say aloud or silently:

"By sweetness and spice, magic and cheer,
These fortunes bring blessings throughout the year.
With love and joy, each cookie's delight,
Reveals the path to wisdom and light."

5. Bake the Cookies

1. Preheat your oven to 375°F (190°C).
2. Spoon small circles of batter (about 1 tablespoon each) onto the parchment-lined baking sheet, spreading them into thin, even circles about 3-4 inches in diameter. Work in small batches, as the cookies must be shaped while warm.
3. Bake for 7-8 minutes, or until the edges turn golden brown.

6. Shape the Fortune Cookies

1. Remove the cookies from the oven and, working quickly, place a fortune strip in the center of each cookie.
2. Fold the cookie in half over the fortune to form a semi-circle. Press the edges lightly to seal.
3. Drape the cookie over the rim of a small cup or bowl to create the iconic crescent shape. Hold it in place for a few seconds until it hardens.
4. Repeat the process with the remaining cookies.

Customizing the Spell for Different Purposes

The Festive Fortune Cookies can be tailored for various magical or celebratory purposes:

1. For Divination

- Write fortunes that answer specific questions or provide guidance, such as:
    - *"The opportunity you seek is near—stay open to it."*
    - *"Look within for the clarity you desire."*

2. For Group Harmony

- Create fortunes that promote peace and connection, such as:
    - *"Together, you will find joy and strength."*
    - *"The bond between you grows brighter each day."*

3. For Manifestation

- Focus the fortunes on personal or collective goals, such as:
    - *"Your dreams are aligning—trust the process."*
    - *"Abundance flows easily into your life."*

4. For Seasonal Blessings

- Use fortunes that align with the festive spirit, such as:
    - *"May your holidays be filled with laughter and love."*
    - *"This season brings unexpected gifts and blessings."*

Enhancing the Magic

- **Infuse with Crystals:** Place clear quartz or citrine near your workspace while crafting the cookies to amplify clarity and joy.
- **Add Magical Symbols:** Decorate the cookies with edible glitter, icing, or symbols that enhance their magical purpose, such as stars for guidance or hearts for love.
- **Incorporate Seasonal Scents:** Use a diffuser with peppermint or cinnamon essential oils to create an uplifting atmosphere while you work.

Sharing the Cookies

When serving or sharing the cookies:

1. Place them in a decorative bowl or tray, and encourage recipients to choose intuitively.
2. Before revealing the fortunes, invite everyone to take a moment of silence, focusing on their question or intention.
3. Remind them that the fortune they receive is meant to guide or uplift them, offering insight aligned with their needs.

Signs of Success

The Festive Fortune Cookies' magic is working when:

- Recipients report feeling uplifted or inspired by their fortunes.
- The cookies' messages align meaningfully with the recipient's current situation or needs.
- A sense of joy and harmony surrounds the sharing of the cookies.

Conclusion

Festive Fortune Cookies are a delightful and versatile way to combine culinary creativity with magical practice. Whether used for divination, blessings, or seasonal joy, these enchanted treats bring guidance and positivity to all who receive them. By crafting them with intention and care, you create not only delicious desserts but also tools for spreading magic and wisdom throughout the holiday season.

Part III: Magical Crafts and Seasonal Enchantments

Chapter 11: Crafting Gingerbread Talismans

Crafting **Gingerbread Talismans** is a powerful and delightful way to create magical tools for blessings and protection. These miniature Gingerbread Golem tokens serve as personal guardians, attracting positive energy, repelling negativity, and infusing spaces with warmth and safety. They are ideal for carrying on your person, placing in key areas of your home, or gifting to loved ones as enchanted charms.

This chapter explores how to craft, empower, and use Gingerbread Talismans, including the symbolism of their design, step-by-step instructions, and tips for amplifying their magical potency.

The Purpose of Gingerbread Talismans

Gingerbread Talismans are versatile magical tools designed for:

- **Personal Protection:** Acting as a portable shield against harmful energy or intentions.
- **Blessings:** Attracting positive outcomes, such as harmony, good fortune, or health.
- **Space Clearing:** Cleansing and protecting specific areas, such as doorways or workspaces.
- **Magical Gifts:** Sharing blessings and protection with others in a tangible, thoughtful way.

By focusing your intention during their creation, these talismans become powerful conduits for magical energy.

Symbolism of Gingerbread Talismans

The talismans draw their power from the symbolic qualities of gingerbread and the traditional shapes used in their design:

- **Gingerbread:** A grounding and protective medium that embodies strength, warmth, and sweetness.
- **Shapes:** The form of the talisman adds a layer of meaning:
    - **Humanoid Figures:** Represent guardianship and connection.
    - **Hearts:** Symbolize love, compassion, and emotional protection.
    - **Stars:** Signify guidance, inspiration, and celestial blessings.
    - **Circles:** Reflect unity, wholeness, and the cyclical nature of protection.

Ingredients and Tools

To craft Gingerbread Talismans, gather the following:

Ingredients

- **For the gingerbread dough:**
    - 2 cups all-purpose flour
    - 1 teaspoon baking soda
    - 1 teaspoon ground ginger (for protection and strength)
    - 1 teaspoon ground cinnamon (for harmony and amplification)
    - ½ teaspoon ground cloves (for sealing and banishing negativity)
    - ½ teaspoon nutmeg (for luck and blessings)
    - ½ cup unsalted butter
    - ½ cup dark brown sugar (for grounding energy)
    - ¼ cup molasses (for resilience and stability)
    - 1 large egg
- **For decoration:**

  - Icing (white or colored)
  - Edible glitter or sugar crystals
  - Small candies or nuts (optional)

Tools

- Gingerbread cookie cutters (shapes of your choice)
- A rolling pin
- A baking sheet lined with parchment paper
- A small paintbrush (optional, for applying sigils or symbols with icing)
- Ribbon or twine (if you plan to hang the talismans)

Step-by-Step Guide to Crafting Gingerbread Talismans
1. Prepare Your Space

- Begin by cleansing your workspace to ensure it is free of distractions and negative energy. Burn sage, rosemary, or cinnamon incense, or sprinkle salt water around the area.
- Set up your tools and ingredients in an orderly manner to create a focused and sacred atmosphere.

2. Make the Gingerbread Dough

1. In a medium bowl, combine the flour, baking soda, ginger, cinnamon, cloves, and nutmeg.
2. In a separate bowl, cream the butter and brown sugar until light and fluffy. Add the molasses and egg, mixing well.
3. Gradually add the dry ingredients to the wet mixture, stirring until a smooth dough forms.
4. Wrap the dough in plastic wrap and chill for 30 minutes to 1 hour. As the dough chills, focus on your intention for the talismans.

3. Roll and Cut the Talismans

1. Preheat your oven to 350°F (175°C).
2. Roll out the dough on a floured surface to about ¼-inch thickness.
3. Use cookie cutters to create shapes that align with your intention. For example:
    - **Humanoid figures** for protection and guardianship.
    - **Hearts** for love and emotional balance.
    - **Stars** for guidance and inspiration.
4. Place the cut shapes onto the prepared baking sheet.

4. Enchant the Dough

1. Before baking, hold your hands over the cookie sheet and focus your energy on the talismans.
2. Say the following incantation (or create your own):

"Gingerbread strong, with spices true,
Protect and bless in all you do.
By my will, your power grows,
To guard, to guide, where'er you go."

1. Visualize each talisman glowing with protective or blessing energy, depending on its intended purpose.

5. Bake the Talismans

1. Bake the cookies for 8–10 minutes, or until the edges are golden brown.
2. Allow the talismans to cool completely before handling.

6. Decorate and Empower

1. Use icing to decorate the talismans with meaningful symbols or sigils:
    - **Protection Sigils:** Create runes or sigils to ward off harm.
    - **Blessing Symbols:** Use hearts, stars, or spirals to represent love, guidance, and positivity.
2. Add edible glitter or sugar crystals to enhance the talismans' visual and magical appeal.
3. As you decorate, focus on imbuing the talismans with your desired energy. Speak your intention aloud for each one.

Using the Gingerbread Talismans
1. Personal Protection

- Carry a small talisman in your pocket or purse to guard against negativity and harmful influences.

2. Home Blessings

- Place talismans near doorways, windows, or altars to create a protective barrier around your space.

3. Gifts of Magic

- Gift talismans to loved ones, sharing their protective or blessing energy. Include a note explaining their magical purpose and how to use them.

4. Ritual Offerings

- Use the talismans as offerings during rituals or meditations to invite blessings or enhance your magical workings.

Enhancing the Magic

- **Add Crystals:** Attach small crystals (e.g., amethyst for protection or rose quartz for love) to the talismans using ribbon or twine.
- **Pair with Aromatics:** Store the talismans with dried herbs like rosemary, lavender, or bay leaves to amplify their magical properties.
- **Recharge Regularly:** Refresh the talismans' energy by placing them in moonlight or near a burning candle during rituals.

Signs of Effectiveness

You'll know your Gingerbread Talismans are working when you notice:

- A heightened sense of protection or peace in the space where they are placed.
- Positive feedback from recipients of gifted talismans.
- A tangible shift in energy, such as a reduction in conflict or an increase in harmonious interactions.

Conclusion

Crafting Gingerbread Talismans is a deeply rewarding practice that combines culinary creativity with magical intention. These enchanted tokens serve as charming and powerful tools for blessings and protection, perfect for personal use or sharing with others. By channeling your energy into their creation and aligning their symbolism with your goals, Gingerbread Talismans become enduring symbols of warmth, safety, and love.

Chapter 12: Edible Altars

An **edible altar** is a sacred space crafted with food and other natural, consumable elements to honor the divine, channel magical energy, and create a harmonious atmosphere. These altars combine the sacred and the earthly, inviting blessings and intentions to flow through the act of creating and sharing food. Unlike traditional altars, edible altars engage all the senses and foster connection to the physical world in a tangible way, making them powerful tools for manifestation, healing, and spiritual alignment.

In this chapter, we will explore how to build and empower an edible altar, using food, spices, and other offerings to create a space of sacred energy. Whether for a ritual, celebration, or personal intention, the edible altar acts as a focal point for your desires, grounding them in the present and inviting divine or natural forces to work in your favor.

Why Build an Edible Altar?

Edible altars provide several benefits, both magical and practical:

- **Tangible Connection:** Incorporating food connects the magical and physical realms, allowing you to "digest" the energy of your work.
- **Symbolic Expression:** Each edible component carries specific meanings and energy, making your altar a powerful representation of your intentions.
- **Sustainability:** Unlike traditional altars, edible altars leave no waste—they're consumed or shared, spreading the magic to all involved.
- **Festive Appeal:** Perfect for holidays and gatherings, edible altars are inclusive, engaging, and aligned with the celebratory spirit of the season.

When to Create an Edible Altar

Edible altars can be crafted for various purposes and occasions, such as:

- **Seasonal Celebrations:** Honor the energy of a specific season or festival (e.g., Yule, Christmas, Winter Solstice).
- **Manifestation Rituals:** Focus on attracting abundance, love, protection, or other intentions.
- **Thanksgiving or Gratitude Ceremonies:** Use the altar to express appreciation and share blessings with others.
- **Personal Devotion:** Create a sacred space to connect with your spiritual path or deities.

The Purpose of an Edible Altar

An edible altar serves several purposes in magical practice:

- **Manifestation:** Focuses your intentions on specific goals by engaging the physical and energetic elements in your ritual work.
- **Blessing and Healing:** Uses food as an offering for blessings, healing, and gratitude.
- **Connection to the Divine:** Honors deities, spirits, or elements, invoking their presence through nourishing and edible offerings.
- **Unity and Gratitude:** Celebrates communal connection, family, and friends, inviting abundance and goodwill into your life and space.

Unlike other types of altars, an edible altar's components are designed to be consumed or shared after the ritual, making it a living, interactive form of magic. It can be used for specific celebrations or personal rituals, combining both the creative act of crafting the altar and the transformative power of food.

Components of an Edible Altar

An edible altar typically consists of food, herbs, spices, and elements that resonate with the intention of the ritual. The following components play key roles in creating an altar that is both sacred and powerful:

1. Food as a Sacred Offering

Food is the foundation of the edible altar. Each ingredient or item should be chosen for its symbolic and magical qualities:

- **Fruits and Vegetables:** Represent the harvest, abundance, and the cyclical nature of life. Apples, oranges, grapes, and pomegranates are often used for their association with fertility and vitality.
- **Breads and Grains:** Symbolize sustenance, grounding, and spiritual nourishment. Fresh-baked bread can represent the body of the Earth, while grains such as rice, wheat, and oats represent prosperity and fertility.
- **Sweet Treats:** Honey, chocolate, and sugar represent sweetness, love, and the sweet side of life, while offering spiritual nourishment.
- **Nuts and Seeds:** Represent potential and growth. They can be offered as symbols of new beginnings or seeds for future goals.
- **Dairy or Vegan Alternatives:** Represent the nurturing and maternal aspects of the divine, offering comfort and emotional sustenance.

2. Herbs and Spices

Herbs and spices have inherent magical properties that can amplify the altar's purpose. Choose herbs and spices based on their correspondences:

- **Cinnamon:** Warming, protective, and prosperity-enhancing.
- **Rosemary:** Healing, purification, and remembrance.
- **Sage:** Purification and cleansing, used to clear space before building the altar.

- **Lavender:** Peace, relaxation, and emotional balance.
- **Thyme:** Courage, strength, and protection.
- **Mint:** Clarity, renewal, and mental stimulation.
- **Basil:** Prosperity, love, and spiritual protection.

Spices like ginger, cloves, nutmeg, and turmeric can be used for invoking energy, power, or purification. These herbs can be sprinkled around the altar or woven into food offerings.

3. Candles

Candles are essential for creating sacred space. They represent light, guidance, and the power of fire. The color of the candle can correspond to the specific intention of the altar:

- **White Candles:** Purity, protection, and divine energy.
- **Red Candles:** Passion, vitality, and courage.
- **Green Candles:** Growth, prosperity, and healing.
- **Gold or Yellow Candles:** Success, abundance, and enlightenment.
- **Purple Candles:** Spiritual power, wisdom, and intuition.

4. Elements of Water and Earth

Water can be used as an offering of purification and flow, while earth elements such as soil or crystals can provide grounding and connection to nature. A small bowl of water or a crystal grid around the altar helps amplify the energetic space.

5. Personal Items or Symbols

To personalize your edible altar, consider incorporating symbols that represent your intentions:

- **Amulets or Tokens:** Small personal items or tokens that represent your goals or desires.
- **Images or Figurines:** Represent deities, ancestors, or spiritual beings you wish to honor or invoke.

- **Sacred Words or Invocations:** Write a phrase, word, or intention and place it near or within the altar to focus your purpose.

Building Your Edible Altar

The process of creating an edible altar can be both meditative and sacred. Follow these steps to craft a space that aligns with your intentions:

1. Clear Your Space

Before you begin assembling your altar, clear the space to ensure the energy is fresh and receptive. Use a cleansing ritual, such as burning sage, palo santo, or using salt water, to purify the area. Light a candle to invite the presence of divine energy.

2. Choose the Altar Location

Select a location for your altar that feels sacred and central to your home. This could be:

- A kitchen counter for cooking-related rituals.
- A dining table for communal blessings and connection.
- A small altar space on a table or shelf to honor your personal goals.

3. Set Your Intentions

Before you begin building the altar, define its purpose. Is it for a personal blessing, healing, or a seasonal celebration? Speak your intention aloud or write it down, placing it at the center of the altar.

4. Arrange the Ingredients

Start by arranging the food offerings on your altar. You can create shapes such as a circle, a spiral, or a simple linear arrangement. Consider placing items that represent abundance, love, health, and protection. For example:

- Arrange fruits in a circular pattern to represent wholeness and completion.

- Use bread or grain offerings as a central focus for the altar, symbolizing sustenance.
- Scatter herbs and spices around the offerings, forming a protective boundary of magic.

5. Add Lighting and Sacred Objects

Place candles around the altar to illuminate the space. Choose colors that align with your intention, such as green for prosperity or white for purity and protection. Place personal symbols, crystals, or images of deities near the food offerings to further empower the space.

6. Empower the Altar

Once the altar is set, sit quietly and center yourself. Focus your energy on the altar, visualizing it glowing with light and vibrant energy. Say a prayer, chant, or speak an affirmation that aligns with the altar's purpose:

"With these offerings, I invite abundance, love, and protection into this space. May the blessings of food, nature, and spirit fill this altar with harmony and peace. So it is."

Focus on your intention for the altar, sending your energy into the food offerings and elements.

Using the Edible Altar

Once the altar is set and empowered, there are many ways to engage with it:

- **Perform Rituals or Ceremonies:** Gather around the altar to perform rituals or prayers, using the food and items on the altar to guide your intentions. This can include meditation, singing, or chanting.
- **Offerings of Gratitude:** Take time to offer thanks for what the altar represents. Share the food with loved ones or consume it mindfully, honoring the blessings it represents.
- **Give and Share:** If you have created the altar as a gift, offer the food to others as a symbolic sharing of blessings.

Maintaining the Edible Altar

Unlike traditional altars that remain untouched, edible altars are meant to be interactive and nourishing. Here are some ways to maintain the altar's energy:

- **Replenish Offerings:** Regularly refresh the food and herbs on your altar to keep it vibrant and full of life.
- **Use Leftovers Creatively:** Use any food leftover from the altar in your daily meals or as part of a communal meal, sharing the blessings and intention of the altar.
- **Cleanse the Altar:** When the ritual is complete or the food has been consumed, clean the altar space and reset it for the next use. You may want to use a gentle cleansing ritual to clear the space before creating a new altar.

Conclusion

An edible altar is a sacred and creative way to connect with the divine, manifest intentions, and celebrate life's blessings. By crafting an altar with food, herbs, and sacred elements, you create a tangible space for healing, growth, and gratitude. Whether used for personal reflection, communal blessings, or honoring the seasons, edible altars invite you to engage with your spirituality through nourishment, love, and intention.

Chapter 13: Spiced Candle Rituals

Candles have been central to magical and spiritual practices for centuries, symbolizing light, transformation, and connection to the divine. When infused with the protective and festive energies of spices, candles become powerful tools for amplifying intentions, shielding spaces, and celebrating the warmth of the holiday season. **Spiced Candle Rituals** merge the elemental power of fire with the magical properties of spices to create a multi-sensory experience that radiates positivity, protection, and festivity.

In this chapter, you will learn how to craft, infuse, and use spiced candles in rituals to manifest your intentions. Whether for protection, harmony, or holiday blessings, these rituals bring a unique charm to your magical practice.

Why Use Spiced Candles in Rituals?

Spiced candles combine the transformative power of fire with the magical properties of spices to create a dynamic and effective ritual tool. Here's why they are so effective:

- **Elemental Energy:** Fire represents transformation, purification, and activation, making it ideal for both protective and celebratory magic.
- **Scent and Symbolism:** Spices like cinnamon, clove, and nutmeg emit powerful aromas that evoke warmth, protection, and holiday cheer, aligning the mind and spirit with the ritual's intention.
- **Customization:** Spiced candles can be tailored to specific intentions, such as banishing negativity, attracting prosperity, or fostering love and unity.

The Magic of Spices in Candle Rituals

Each spice brings its unique energy and symbolism to a ritual. Here are some common spices and their magical properties:

Protective Spices

- **Cinnamon:** Warming, energizing, and protective, cinnamon strengthens intentions and wards off negativity.
- **Clove:** Known for its ability to banish harmful influences, clove creates a shield of safety and security.
- **Ginger:** Adds fiery protection, courage, and empowerment to the candle's energy.

Prosperity and Blessing Spices

- **Nutmeg:** Associated with abundance, luck, and blessings, nutmeg enhances the candle's ability to attract positive outcomes.
- **Star Anise:** Symbolizes clarity, guidance, and good fortune, amplifying the candle's manifestation powers.
- **Allspice:** Combines the energies of protection and prosperity, making it a versatile choice for festive rituals.

Harmonizing Spices

- **Lavender (dried):** Fosters peace, emotional balance, and relaxation, making it ideal for calming rituals.
- **Rosemary:** Clears negativity and promotes mental clarity, aligning the ritual with harmony and focus.
- **Peppermint:** Refreshes and revitalizes, aligning the mind and spirit with renewal and unity.

Crafting Your Spiced Candles

To use spiced candles in rituals, you can either purchase plain candles and infuse them with spices or create your own candles from scratch. Below are detailed instructions for both approaches.

Option 1: Infusing Pre-Made Candles
Materials:

- Plain white, red, or green candles (choose colors based on your intention)
- A selection of ground or dried spices (e.g., cinnamon, clove, nutmeg, rosemary)
- Olive oil or melted coconut oil (to help the spices adhere)
- A small bowl
- A spoon or soft brush

Steps:

1. **Cleanse the Candle:**
   - Wipe the candle with a damp cloth to remove any residue. Hold it in your hands and focus on clearing it of any lingering energy. You can say:

"I cleanse this candle of all energies past,
To hold my intention from first to last."

1. **Prepare the Spice Blend:**
   - In a small bowl, mix your chosen spices. For example:
     - **Protection Blend:** Cinnamon, clove, and ginger.
     - **Abundance Blend:** Nutmeg, star anise, and allspice.
     - **Harmony Blend:** Rosemary, lavender, and peppermint.

2. **Anoint the Candle:**
    ◦ Dip your fingers or a brush into the oil and coat the candle lightly. Roll the candle in the spice blend, ensuring an even coating. As you do this, focus on your intention, visualizing the energy of the spices infusing the candle.
3. **Empower the Candle:**
    ◦ Hold the candle between your hands and visualize it glowing with the energy of your intention. Say aloud:

"By spice and fire, this candle I bless,
To shield, to guide, and bring success.
With every spark, its power grows,
Protect, provide, and overflow."

Option 2: Making Spiced Candles from Scratch
Materials:

- Candle wax (beeswax or soy wax)
- Wicks
- Candle molds or jars
- A double boiler or heat-safe container for melting wax
- Your chosen spices (ground or whole)
- Essential oils (optional, for added scent)
- A skewer or chopstick for holding the wick in place

Steps:

1. **Melt the Wax:**
    ◦ Use a double boiler to melt the wax over low heat. Stir occasionally to ensure it melts evenly.
2. **Prepare the Molds:**
    ◦ Place the wick in the center of the mold or jar, using a skewer to hold it upright.
3. **Add Spices and Oils:**

- Once the wax is fully melted, stir in your chosen spices. You can also add a few drops of essential oil to enhance the scent. Stir clockwise while focusing on your intention.

4. **Pour the Wax:**
   - Carefully pour the wax into the mold or jar, ensuring the wick remains centered.

5. **Cool and Empower:**
   - Allow the candle to cool completely. Once hardened, hold the candle and charge it with your intention using the same empowerment chant provided above.

Spiced Candle Rituals for Protection and Festivity

Once your candles are prepared, you can use them in a variety of rituals. Below are detailed examples:

1. The Protective Flame Ritual

This ritual creates a shield of safety around your home or space.

What You'll Need:

- A spiced candle infused with cinnamon, clove, and ginger
- A bowl of salt
- A small mirror (to reflect negativity away)

Steps:

1. Place the candle in the center of your altar or workspace.
2. Surround the candle with a ring of salt and place the mirror behind it, facing outward.
3. Light the candle and say:

"Flame of fire, spice and might,
Protect this space both day and night.
No harm may enter, no ill shall stay,
This sacred shield begins today."

1. Let the candle burn for at least 15 minutes, visualizing its light forming a protective barrier around you.

2. The Festive Blessing Ritual

This ritual invokes holiday blessings of joy, abundance, and unity.

What You'll Need:

- A spiced candle infused with nutmeg, star anise, and cinnamon
- A small dish of dried fruit or nuts
- A piece of paper and a pen

Steps:

1. Write your blessings or intentions for the season on the paper.
2. Place the candle in the center of the dish and surround it with dried fruit or nuts.
3. Light the candle and say:

"By this flame, blessings flow,
Love and joy, to all I know.
Abundance bright, through season's cheer,
Prosperity comes this blessed year."

1. Allow the candle to burn while you reflect on your intentions.

Maintaining and Enhancing Candle Energy

- **Daily Reaffirmation:** Relight your spiced candles daily to reinforce their energy.
- **Pair with Crystals:** Place crystals like clear quartz, amethyst, or citrine around the candles to amplify their effects.
- **Dispose Respectfully:** When the candle has burned down completely, dispose of the remains respectfully, such as burying them in your garden.

Conclusion

Spiced Candle Rituals offer a beautiful way to combine fire's transformative power with the magical properties of spices. By crafting and empowering these candles, you create tools that bring protection, prosperity, and joy to your rituals and spaces. Whether used during the holidays or throughout the year, spiced candles are a versatile and enchanting addition to your magical practice.

Chapter 14: Gingerbread Wreath Spell

The **Gingerbread Wreath Spell** is a creative and powerful way to combine the charm of holiday decor with protective magic. Wreaths have long been symbolic of unity, eternity, and protection, and when crafted with gingerbread and magical intention, they become potent tools for safeguarding your home and radiating warmth and positivity. This spell walks you through how to weave a wreath imbued with protective magic, using gingerbread, spices, and other seasonal elements.

This chapter provides an extensive guide to crafting a gingerbread wreath, empowering it with magical energy, and using it as both a decorative piece and a magical shield.

The Symbolism of Wreaths and Gingerbread

The wreath, a circular shape with no beginning or end, represents eternity, the cyclical nature of life, and the protective boundary of the home. When combined with gingerbread's grounding and protective properties, the wreath becomes a magical talisman that:

- **Protects the Home:** Creates a barrier against negativity, ill intentions, and harmful influences.
- **Attracts Positivity:** Invites blessings, harmony, and warmth into the household.
- **Celebrates Unity:** Serves as a symbol of togetherness and community during the holiday season.

Ingredients and Materials

To create your Gingerbread Wreath, gather the following:

For the Gingerbread Wreath Base:

- 2 cups all-purpose flour
- 1 teaspoon baking soda
- 1 teaspoon ground cinnamon (for harmony and protection)
- 1 teaspoon ground ginger (for strength and grounding)
- ½ teaspoon ground nutmeg (for blessings and abundance)
- ½ teaspoon ground cloves (for banishing negativity)
- ½ cup unsalted butter, softened
- ½ cup dark brown sugar (for stability and grounding)
- ¼ cup molasses (for resilience)
- 1 large egg
- Circular templates (e.g., a round baking pan or a wreath-shaped mold)

For Decoration:

- Royal icing (to bind and decorate the wreath)
- Edible glitter or sugar crystals
- Small candies, nuts, or dried fruit (for embellishment)
- Ribbon or twine (optional, for hanging)

For Empowerment:

- A small white or gold candle
- A sprinkle of salt (for purification)
- Cinnamon sticks or dried rosemary sprigs (for added protection)

Step-by-Step Guide to Crafting the Gingerbread Wreath
1. Prepare Your Space

1. Begin by cleansing your workspace to remove any lingering negativity. Use your preferred method, such as burning sage, sprinkling salt water, or visualizing white light filling the area.
2. Set up your ingredients and tools, ensuring you have everything within reach.

2. Make the Gingerbread Dough

1. In a medium bowl, combine the flour, baking soda, cinnamon, ginger, nutmeg, and cloves.
2. In a separate bowl, cream the butter and brown sugar until light and fluffy. Add the molasses and egg, mixing well.
3. Gradually add the dry ingredients to the wet mixture, stirring until a smooth dough forms.
4. Wrap the dough in plastic wrap and chill for at least 30 minutes. As the dough rests, focus on your intention for the wreath, visualizing it as a protective shield for your home.

3. Shape the Wreath Base

1. Preheat your oven to 350°F (175°C).
2. Roll out the dough on a floured surface to about ¼-inch thickness.
3. Use circular templates to cut out the wreath base. You can create an outer circle using a large bowl or baking pan and an inner circle using a smaller item, such as a cup or cookie cutter, to form the ring shape.
4. If desired, cut out small gingerbread shapes (e.g., stars, hearts, or people) to decorate the wreath.

4. Bake the Gingerbread

1. Place the wreath base and any additional shapes onto a baking sheet lined with parchment paper.
2. Bake for 10–12 minutes, or until the edges are golden brown. Allow the pieces to cool completely before handling.

5. Assemble and Decorate the Wreath

1. Use royal icing to attach the decorative shapes (e.g., stars or hearts) to the wreath base. As you apply each piece, focus on its protective symbolism:
   - **Stars:** Guidance and inspiration.
   - **Hearts:** Love and emotional harmony.
   - **Figures:** Guardianship and connection.
2. Add embellishments like edible glitter, candies, or nuts to enhance the wreath's beauty and magical potency.
3. Tie a ribbon or twine to the wreath for hanging, if desired.

Empowering the Gingerbread Wreath

Once the wreath is crafted and decorated, it's time to infuse it with protective magic.

1. Light the Candle

- Place the wreath on a clean surface or altar and light a small white or gold candle nearby.
- Focus on the candle's flame, visualizing its light surrounding the wreath with protective energy.

2. Cleanse the Wreath

- Sprinkle a pinch of salt over the wreath while saying:

"By salt and spice, this wreath I seal,
To guard this home with strength and zeal."

3. Add Protective Herbs

- Place cinnamon sticks or dried rosemary sprigs around the wreath to amplify its protective energy. Say:

"Cinnamon strong and rosemary true,
Protect this space in all I do."

4. Speak Your Intention

- Place your hands over the wreath and focus your energy on its purpose. Speak your intention aloud, such as:

"This wreath of gingerbread and spice,
Guards this home from all that's vice.
Let blessings flow and joy increase,
This space is safe, with love and peace."

Using the Gingerbread Wreath

After empowering the wreath, hang or display it in a prominent location, such as:

- **The Front Door:** To act as a protective barrier against negativity entering your home.
- **Above the Fireplace:** To radiate warmth and blessings throughout your living space.
- **In a Sacred Space:** To anchor the energy of protection and harmony in your home.

Tips for Maintaining the Wreath's Energy

- **Refresh the Spell:** Periodically recharge the wreath's energy by lighting a candle nearby and reaffirming your intention.
- **Replace Decorations:** If any part of the wreath becomes damaged, replace it with fresh decorations to maintain its symbolic integrity.
- **Respectfully Dispose:** When the holiday season ends, dispose of the wreath respectfully by returning it to nature (e.g., burying or composting) or by burning it in a ceremonial fire to release its energy.

Customizing the Wreath Spell

The Gingerbread Wreath Spell is highly adaptable. Consider these variations based on your needs:

- **For Abundance:** Add symbols of prosperity, such as gold or green icing, dried orange slices, or coins.
- **For Love and Unity:** Incorporate heart-shaped decorations and pink or red accents.
- **For Spiritual Connection:** Use star shapes, clear quartz, or purple decorations to align the wreath with higher wisdom.

Conclusion

The Gingerbread Wreath Spell is a beautiful and practical way to combine festive tradition with magical intention. By weaving a wreath imbued with protective energy, you create not only a decorative piece but also a magical shield that safeguards your home and invites blessings. Whether displayed at your front door or in a sacred space, the gingerbread wreath serves as a tangible reminder of the warmth, unity, and magic of the season.

Chapter 15: Festive Incense and Oils

Aromatic blends of incense and oils have been used for centuries to enhance magical rituals, cleanse spaces, and invoke protective spirits. For the Gingerbread Golem, these blends are powerful tools to summon its protective essence, fortify its energy, and create a harmonious environment filled with festive warmth. The carefully chosen ingredients—spices, resins, and essential oils—align with the Golem's qualities of strength, sweetness, and resilience, making these recipes perfect for seasonal rituals and magical workings.

In this chapter, you will learn how to craft incense and oils that invoke the Gingerbread Golem's protective spirit. These blends can be used to enhance spells, purify spaces, or simply bring a touch of magic to your holiday celebrations.

The Power of Aromatics in Magic

Aromatic materials like spices, herbs, and resins carry potent magical properties, amplified when burned as incense or blended into oils. Their scents not only affect the physical senses but also influence the energy of spaces and individuals.

Why Use Festive Incense and Oils?

- **Protection:** Burn incense to ward off negative energy and invite the Golem's protective spirit.
- **Connection:** Use oils to anoint candles, tools, or yourself, deepening your connection to the Golem.
- **Atmosphere:** Create a warm, magical environment filled with festive and harmonious energy.

Magical Ingredients for Festive Blends

Each ingredient used in the incense and oils serves a purpose aligned with the Gingerbread Golem's protective and festive qualities:

Resins

- **Frankincense:** Elevates spiritual energy, purifies spaces, and invites blessings.
- **Myrrh:** Grounds and stabilizes energy, offering deep protection and resilience.
- **Copal:** Clears negativity and enhances connection to higher energies.

Herbs and Spices

- **Cinnamon:** Warming, protective, and amplifies magical intentions.
- **Clove:** Repels negativity and provides a shield of safety.
- **Ginger:** Fiery and empowering, it adds strength and courage.
- **Nutmeg:** Brings blessings, prosperity, and good fortune.
- **Star Anise:** Promotes clarity, guidance, and a connection to celestial energies.

Essential Oils

- **Peppermint Oil:** Refreshes and revitalizes energy, aligning the mind and spirit.
- **Orange Oil:** Invites joy, prosperity, and festive cheer.
- **Vanilla Oil:** Promotes sweetness, warmth, and harmony.
- **Cedarwood Oil:** Grounds energy and strengthens protective boundaries.

Recipes for Festive Incense

1. Protective Gingerbread Incense

This loose incense blend invokes the Gingerbread Golem's protective spirit, creating a shield of warmth and safety.

Ingredients:

- 1 tablespoon ground cinnamon
- 1 teaspoon ground clove
- 1 teaspoon ground ginger
- ½ teaspoon ground nutmeg
- 1 teaspoon frankincense resin
- 1 teaspoon myrrh resin
- 1 star anise pod, crushed

Instructions:

1. Combine all the ingredients in a small bowl, focusing on your intention as you mix. Visualize the Gingerbread Golem standing guard over your space.
2. Store the mixture in an airtight container until ready to use.
3. Burn a small pinch of the incense on a charcoal disc in a heatproof bowl or censer, allowing the aromatic smoke to fill your space.

Best Uses:

- Before rituals to purify and protect the area.
- During meditation to connect with the Golem's spirit.
- As a daily cleansing tool for your home.

2. Festive Harmony Incense

This blend combines protective energy with the joyous and unifying qualities of the holiday season.

Ingredients:

- 2 tablespoons dried orange peel, crushed
- 1 teaspoon ground cinnamon
- 1 teaspoon ground ginger
- 1 teaspoon copal resin
- ½ teaspoon dried peppermint
- ½ teaspoon dried rosemary

Instructions:

1. Blend the ingredients in a mortar and pestle or bowl, visualizing harmony and protection flowing through the mixture.
2. Burn on a charcoal disc to invite a festive, magical atmosphere into your space.

Best Uses:

- During family gatherings to promote unity and peace.
- When setting up holiday decorations to imbue your home with protective joy.

Recipes for Festive Oils
1. Gingerbread Protection Oil
This oil channels the Golem's essence, combining warming spices and grounding oils to create a powerful protective blend.
Ingredients:

- 4 tablespoons carrier oil (e.g., almond, jojoba, or coconut oil)
- 5 drops cinnamon essential oil
- 3 drops clove essential oil
- 2 drops ginger essential oil
- 2 drops frankincense essential oil
- 1 small piece of star anise

Instructions:

1. Add the carrier oil to a small glass bottle or jar.
2. Drop in the essential oils, one at a time, focusing on your intention of protection.
3. Place the piece of star anise into the bottle as a talismanic addition.
4. Seal the bottle and gently swirl it to mix the ingredients.

Best Uses:

- Anoint candles before spells or rituals.
- Dab onto your wrists or temples for personal protection.
- Use to bless doorways and windows for home protection.

2. Festive Blessing Oil

This oil blend is designed to attract joy, harmony, and abundance while invoking the warmth of the holiday season.

Ingredients:

- 4 tablespoons carrier oil (e.g., almond, jojoba, or olive oil)
- 4 drops orange essential oil
- 3 drops vanilla essential oil
- 3 drops cinnamon essential oil
- 2 drops nutmeg essential oil
- 1 small dried orange peel segment

Instructions:

1. Combine the carrier oil and essential oils in a glass bottle, swirling gently to blend.
2. Add the dried orange peel to the bottle as a symbol of joy and abundance.
3. Seal the bottle and store in a cool, dark place when not in use.

Best Uses:

- Anoint yourself or others during holiday blessings.
- Use to dress altar candles for rituals focused on gratitude or abundance.
- Apply to the edges of holiday cards or gifts to imbue them with magical energy.

Enhancing the Magic of Incense and Oils

1. Set Clear Intentions

Before crafting or using incense and oils, take a moment to clearly define your intention. Whether it's protection, harmony, or abundance, focusing on your purpose enhances the potency of the blends.

2. Charge the Blends

Hold the finished incense or oil in your hands and visualize it glowing with magical energy. Speak a blessing or incantation to empower it, such as:

"By spice and scent, this blend I bless,
To guard, to guide, to bring success.
Protective warmth, sweet harmony,
Fill this space with magic free."

3. Store with Care

Keep your incense and oils in airtight containers, stored in a cool, dark place. Label them with their purpose and the date they were created.

4. Pair with Ritual Tools

Use the incense and oils in conjunction with candles, crystals, or Gingerbread Golem talismans for amplified magical effects.

Conclusion

Festive Incense and Oils are potent and versatile tools for invoking the Gingerbread Golem's protective spirit and enhancing the energy of your rituals. By blending the warming and grounding properties of spices, resins, and essential oils, you create aromatic allies that shield your space, invite blessings, and infuse your home with the magic of the season. Whether used for personal rituals or shared with loved ones, these blends connect you to the sacred and joyful energy of the holidays.

Part IV: Advanced Gingerbread Magicks

Chapter 16: Sweet Manifestation Rituals

The power of food in magic lies not only in its sustenance but also in its ability to channel energy and intention. **Sweet Manifestation Rituals** use baked goods as focal points to bring desires to fruition. These rituals combine the transformative process of baking with the power of visualization and intention-setting, making them a practical and delicious way to manifest your goals. By crafting and infusing baked goods with magical energy, you create edible tools that carry your desires into the world, allowing the act of eating to symbolize receiving and embodying your manifestations.

This chapter will provide detailed guidance on how to use baked goods—such as cookies, cakes, and bread—as vessels for your magical intentions, along with step-by-step instructions for performing Sweet Manifestation Rituals.

Why Use Baked Goods for Manifestation?

Baked goods are uniquely suited for manifestation magic because:

- **Transformation:** The process of baking—combining ingredients, applying heat, and creating something new—mirrors the manifestation process of turning desires into reality.
- **Sweetness:** Sugar and other sweet ingredients attract positivity, joy, and abundance, amplifying the energy of your desires.
- **Grounding Energy:** Flour, grains, and other base ingredients provide grounding energy, anchoring your intentions in the physical world.
- **Symbolism:** Specific baked goods can represent different desires (e.g., a round loaf for completeness or cookies for sharing abundance).

Key Elements of Sweet Manifestation Rituals

Before diving into recipes and rituals, it's important to understand the magical elements that make baked goods effective tools for manifestation:

1. Ingredients and Their Magical Properties

Each ingredient carries unique energy that contributes to your intention:

- **Flour:** Stability, grounding, and the foundation of your goal.
- **Sugar or Honey:** Sweetens the outcome and attracts positivity.
- **Spices:** Add layers of magical energy based on their properties:
    - Cinnamon: Prosperity and success.
    - Nutmeg: Luck and blessings.
    - Clove: Protection and strength.
    - Ginger: Energy and empowerment.
- **Butter or Oil:** Adds richness, symbolizing abundance.
- **Eggs:** Represent new beginnings and the birth of desires.
- **Milk or Dairy Alternatives:** Nurturing energy that sustains and supports your manifestations.

2. Shapes and Symbols

The shape of your baked goods can enhance their magical intention:

- **Circles:** Unity, completeness, and wholeness.
- **Stars:** Guidance, inspiration, and celestial blessings.
- **Hearts:** Love, compassion, and emotional desires.
- **Braids (e.g., in bread):** Intertwining energies, relationships, or paths.

3. Timing

Perform your Sweet Manifestation Rituals during specific moon phases or times of day for added potency:

- **New Moon:** For setting new intentions or manifesting beginnings.
- **Waxing Moon:** For growth and attraction.
- **Full Moon:** For completion and abundance.
- **Morning:** To align with fresh starts and new energy.

Step-by-Step Sweet Manifestation Ritual

This general ritual can be applied to any baked good recipe, making it versatile for different desires.

1. Choose Your Intention

- Clearly define what you want to manifest. Write it down on a piece of paper in the present tense as though it has already happened. For example:
    ◦ *"I am financially abundant and secure."*
    ◦ *"My relationships are harmonious and filled with love."*

2. Prepare Your Space

- Clean your kitchen or workspace to ensure it's free of distractions and negative energy.
- Light a white or gold candle to symbolize clarity and success.
- Play calming or uplifting music, or work in silence to focus your intention.

3. Infuse Ingredients with Intention

- As you measure and mix each ingredient, focus on its symbolic meaning and how it contributes to your goal. For example:
    ◦ While adding flour, say: *"This flour forms the stable foundation of my desire."*
    ◦ While adding sugar, say: *"This sweetness attracts positivity and joy into my life."*
    ◦ While adding spices, say: *"These spices empower my goal with energy and protection."*

4. Chant or Visualize While Mixing

- As you mix the ingredients, visualize your desire as though it has already manifested. Imagine yourself experiencing the outcome you want, feeling the emotions associated with success.
- Chant a simple affirmation or rhyme to focus your energy. For example:

"By sweetness and spice, my will takes flight,
My dreams come true, both day and night."

5. Shape with Purpose

- Shape the dough or batter in a way that reflects your intention (e.g., forming a circle for unity or using cookie cutters to create symbolic shapes).
- If desired, carve or draw symbols, sigils, or words into the dough to amplify its energy.

6. Bake with Focus

- Place the baked goods in the oven and visualize the heat activating your intention, transforming it from a thought into a tangible reality.
- While the goods bake, meditate on your goal or perform additional spellwork.

7. Empower the Final Product

- Once the baked goods have cooled, hold them in your hands and speak your intention aloud. For example:

"By the magic of transformation and the sweetness of life,
These treats carry my desire into reality. So it is."

8. Consume or Share

- Eat the baked goods mindfully, savoring each bite as a symbol of receiving your manifestation.
- Alternatively, share them with others (if your intention involves communal goals, like harmony or abundance) to spread the energy.

Magical Recipes for Sweet Manifestation
1. Cinnamon Prosperity Rolls
These rolls are perfect for manifesting financial success and abundance.

Ingredients:

- 2 ¾ cups all-purpose flour
- 1 packet instant yeast
- ½ cup warm milk
- 3 tablespoons granulated sugar
- 3 tablespoons melted butter
- 1 egg
- 2 teaspoons ground cinnamon
- ¼ cup brown sugar (for filling)

Intention: Focus on financial stability and prosperity as you prepare and roll the dough.
Shaping: Roll the dough into a spiral to symbolize the continual flow of abundance.

2. Star-Shaped Sugar Cookies

These cookies are ideal for manifesting guidance, inspiration, and clarity.

Ingredients:

- 2 ½ cups all-purpose flour
- 1 cup unsalted butter, softened
- 1 cup sugar
- 1 egg
- 1 teaspoon vanilla extract
- Edible glitter or sugar crystals (for decoration)

Intention: Focus on receiving clarity or guidance in your life while cutting the dough into star shapes.

Decoration: Sprinkle edible glitter to symbolize the light of inspiration.

3. Heartwarming Gingerbread Cake

This rich and spicy cake is ideal for manifesting love, harmony, and emotional healing.

Ingredients:

- 2 ½ cups all-purpose flour
- 1 teaspoon baking soda
- 2 teaspoons ground ginger
- 1 teaspoon ground cinnamon
- ½ teaspoon ground cloves
- ½ cup molasses
- ½ cup butter, melted
- 1 cup brown sugar
- 2 eggs
- 1 cup hot water

Intention: Focus on love and emotional well-being while mixing and pouring the batter.

Decoration: Drizzle icing in heart shapes to reinforce your intention.

Tips for Success

1. **Be Present:** The more focus and intention you bring to the ritual, the more effective it will be.
2. **Taste the Magic:** As you eat the baked goods, visualize your desire coming to life. Treat each bite as an act of receiving your manifestation.
3. **Share the Joy:** If sharing with others, explain the magic behind the treats to amplify their collective energy.
4. **Use Correspondences:** Align the timing, colors, and ingredients of your ritual with your goal for added potency.

Conclusion

Sweet Manifestation Rituals are a creative and delicious way to align your intentions with the transformative power of magic. By using the process of baking as a metaphor for manifesting desires, you combine practical action with focused energy to bring your goals into reality. Whether creating prosperity rolls, star cookies, or heartwarming cakes, these rituals turn everyday baking into an act of magic, making your dreams both tangible and attainable.

Chapter 17: Binding Through Sweetness

The act of binding through sweetness is an ancient and gentle magical technique that uses sweet ingredients, such as honey, sugar, and spices, to mend relationships, foster harmony, and resolve conflicts. Unlike coercive binding spells, **Binding Through Sweetness** focuses on creating mutual understanding, affection, and goodwill, allowing all parties involved to benefit from the positive energy of the spell.

This chapter will guide you through the history, purpose, and step-by-step techniques of sweetening magic, providing you with tools to strengthen bonds, heal emotional rifts, and promote harmonious connections.

The Philosophy of Sweet Binding

Sweetening magic operates on the principle that like attracts like: by infusing sweetness into your magical work, you draw sweetness, love, and understanding into your relationships. This type of magic is especially effective for:

- **Resolving Conflicts:** Dissolving misunderstandings and replacing negativity with compassion.
- **Strengthening Bonds:** Deepening connections between friends, family, or romantic partners.
- **Creating Peace:** Promoting harmony in tense or challenging situations.
- **Encouraging Cooperation:** Inspiring collaboration and mutual respect in personal or professional relationships.

Magical Ingredients for Sweet Binding

The success of sweet binding spells depends on the energy and symbolism of the ingredients used. Here are some commonly used ingredients and their magical properties:

Sweeteners

- **Honey:** Represents long-lasting sweetness, love, and the ability to "stick" people or energies together harmoniously.
- **Sugar:** Attracts positivity, joy, and lightness to relationships.
- **Brown Sugar:** Adds grounding and stability to the spell while maintaining sweetness.
- **Molasses:** Symbolizes patience, deep understanding, and resilience in relationships.

Spices

- **Cinnamon:** Adds warmth, passion, and protection to the relationship.
- **Nutmeg:** Attracts luck, blessings, and a harmonious flow of energy.
- **Clove:** Strengthens bonds and ensures loyalty.
- **Ginger:** Brings energy and empowerment to resolve issues quickly and effectively.

Other Ingredients

- **Vanilla:** Promotes harmony, comfort, and emotional healing.
- **Rose Petals:** Symbolize love, beauty, and emotional connection.
- **Lavender:** Brings calm, peace, and clarity to tense situations.

When to Perform Sweet Binding Spells

Timing can enhance the effectiveness of sweetening spells:

- **Waxing Moon:** Ideal for growth and strengthening bonds.
- **Full Moon:** Best for emotional healing and resolving conflicts.
- **Fridays:** Associated with Venus, the planet of love and harmony.
- **Morning Hours:** Aligns with new beginnings and fresh energy.

Preparing for Sweet Binding Spells

1. Clear Your Intentions

Before performing any spell, take time to reflect on your intentions. Be specific about the outcome you desire and ensure your intentions are ethical and positive. For example:

- Instead of: *"I want [person] to agree with everything I say,"* focus on: *"I want mutual understanding and open communication."*

2. Cleanse Your Space

Clear your space of negativity using a cleansing ritual, such as burning sage or sprinkling salt water. This ensures your spellwork begins in a space of clarity and focus.

3. Gather Personal Items (Optional)

If working on a specific relationship, you may include personal items that symbolize the connection, such as photographs, letters, or small objects associated with the individual(s).

Sweet Binding Techniques
1. The Honey Jar Spell
This classic spell is one of the most effective and versatile sweetening techniques.
What You'll Need:

- A small jar with a lid
- Honey (or molasses for a slower, deeper approach)
- A piece of paper and pen
- A pink or white candle
- Optional: Cinnamon, rose petals, or lavender

Instructions:

1. **Write Your Intention:**
   - On a piece of paper, write the name of the person (or people) you want to sweeten. Beneath their name, write your specific intention, such as *"May our communication be filled with kindness and understanding."*
2. **Prepare the Jar:**
   - Place the paper inside the jar. Add honey to cover the paper completely, visualizing the sweetness of honey infusing the relationship.
3. **Add Optional Ingredients:**
   - Add a pinch of cinnamon, rose petals, or lavender to enhance the spell's energy.
4. **Seal and Empower:**
   - Seal the jar and hold it between your hands. Visualize the relationship blossoming with warmth, love, and harmony.
5. **Light the Candle:**

- Place the jar on your altar or a safe surface. Light a pink or white candle and let a few drops of wax seal the jar's lid. Say:

"Honey sweet, this bond I mend,
Love and harmony, let it extend.
By this spell, goodwill takes flight,
Sweetness grows both day and night."

1. **Store the Jar:**
   - Keep the jar in a safe place and revisit it weekly by lighting another candle to reinforce the spell.

2. Sweetened Baked Goods

Infuse baked treats with magic to sweeten relationships or resolve conflicts.

What You'll Need:

- A recipe for cookies, cakes, or bread
- Ingredients associated with love and harmony (e.g., cinnamon, sugar, vanilla)
- A piece of parchment paper

Instructions:

1. **Set Your Intention:**
   - Before baking, write your intention on a piece of parchment paper. Place it under the mixing bowl or baking pan as you prepare the recipe.
2. **Infuse the Ingredients:**
   - As you measure and mix each ingredient, focus on its symbolic energy. For example:
     - *"This sugar brings sweetness to our bond."*
     - *"This cinnamon adds warmth and protection to our connection."*
3. **Bake and Share:**
   - Bake the goods with love and intention. Share them with the person or group you want to sweeten, visualizing harmony and understanding as they enjoy the treats.

3. Sweet Water Sprinkling

This simple ritual uses sweetened water to diffuse negativity and promote peace in your environment.

What You'll Need:

- A small bowl of water
- 1 tablespoon sugar or honey
- A pinch of cinnamon
- Optional: Lavender or rose water

Instructions:

1. **Mix the Sweet Water:**
   - Combine the ingredients in a bowl, stirring clockwise while focusing on your intention.
2. **Sprinkle the Water:**
   - Dip your fingers into the sweetened water and sprinkle it around your space, especially in areas where tension is high. As you do, say:

"By sweetness and spice, peace shall reign,
All negativity shall wane.
Harmony flows, love takes its place,
Sweet blessings fill this sacred space."

1. **Use as Needed:**
   - Repeat this ritual whenever you feel the energy needs balancing.

Signs the Spell is Working

You may notice the following signs that your sweet binding spell is taking effect:

- Improved communication and understanding in the relationship.
- A noticeable reduction in tension or conflict.
- Feelings of warmth and connection between you and the other person(s).

Maintaining the Energy

- **Refresh the Spell:** Revisit and reinforce your sweet binding work regularly, especially if the relationship is ongoing or the situation evolves.
- **Show Gratitude:** Acknowledge the progress and improvements in your relationship, expressing gratitude for the magic at work.
- **Pair with Actions:** Sweetening magic works best when paired with kind words, thoughtful gestures, and genuine effort in the relationship.

Conclusion

Binding Through Sweetness is a gentle yet effective way to sweeten relationships, resolve conflicts, and foster harmony. By using honey, sugar, and spices in thoughtful rituals, you can channel the magic of sweetness to heal emotional rifts, strengthen bonds, and create lasting peace. These techniques remind us that magic is not just about casting spells—it's about infusing our actions and intentions with love, compassion, and understanding.

Chapter 18: The Frosting Veil

The **Frosting Veil** is a spell designed to enhance psychic visions, strengthen intuitive abilities, and deepen dream work. Drawing from the cooling, reflective qualities of frosting, this spell uses its smooth, transformative nature as a metaphorical "veil" between the physical and spiritual realms. By preparing and empowering frosting as part of a ritual, you can create a magical tool that helps open your third eye, strengthen dream recall, and bring clarity to your visions.

This chapter provides detailed guidance on crafting and using the Frosting Veil spell, incorporating both practical and magical elements for an immersive experience.

The Concept of the Frosting Veil

The frosting in this spell symbolizes a soft, sweet barrier between the physical and spiritual worlds. Much like a veil, it obscures while also revealing—helping to bridge the gap between conscious awareness and intuitive insights. This spell works by:

- **Enhancing Psychic Visions:** Invoking clarity and depth in your intuitive practices, such as scrying or meditation.
- **Strengthening Dream Work:** Promoting vivid dreams, enhancing recall, and opening the gateway to subconscious messages.
- **Creating a Reflective State:** Encouraging a calm, meditative mind ideal for spiritual exploration.

Magical Ingredients for the Frosting Veil Spell

Each ingredient in this spell carries symbolic and magical properties to amplify its effectiveness:

For the Frosting:

- **Powdered Sugar:** Represents clarity, sweetness, and the ability to "see" with precision.
- **Milk or Plant-Based Alternative:** Symbolizes nurturing energy and spiritual flow.
- **Vanilla Extract:** Enhances harmony and connection to higher realms.
- **Food Coloring (Optional):** Use colors like purple (spirituality), blue (calm intuition), or white (clarity and purity) to align with your intention.

For Empowerment:

- **Dried Lavender:** Encourages relaxation, dream work, and psychic receptivity.
- **Ground Star Anise:** Amplifies psychic abilities and aids in divination.
- **Cinnamon:** Adds protective energy and ensures safe exploration of the spiritual realms.
- **Moon Water (Optional):** Infuses the frosting with lunar energy, ideal for psychic and dream work.

When to Perform the Frosting Veil Spell

The timing of this spell can enhance its potency:

- **Full Moon:** For maximizing psychic power and dream clarity.
- **Waxing Crescent Moon:** To build intuitive strength and prepare for deeper exploration.
- **Nighttime:** To align with the natural rhythm of dream work and introspection.

Step-by-Step Guide to the Frosting Veil Spell
1. Set Your Intention
Before beginning, reflect on what you wish to achieve with this spell. Examples of intentions include:

- *"I enhance my psychic visions and gain clarity in my intuitive practices."*
- *"I open myself to dream messages and improve dream recall."*

Write your intention on a piece of paper and keep it nearby as you work.

2. Prepare the Frosting
Ingredients:

- 2 cups powdered sugar
- 2–3 tablespoons milk or plant-based alternative
- 1 teaspoon vanilla extract
- Optional: A few drops of food coloring

Instructions:

1. In a mixing bowl, combine the powdered sugar, milk, and vanilla extract. Stir until the frosting reaches a smooth, spreadable consistency.
2. If desired, add food coloring to align the frosting with your intention.

3. Infuse the Frosting with Magical Energy

- **Add Herbs and Spices:**
    - Sprinkle a small pinch of dried lavender, ground star anise, and cinnamon into the frosting. As you do, visualize their

energies enhancing your psychic abilities and creating a protective veil.

- **Charge the Frosting:**
    - Hold your hands over the bowl and focus on your intention. Visualize a soft, shimmering veil of energy forming around the frosting, glowing with the colors of your intention. Say:

"Frosting sweet, veil so clear,
Open the gates, bring visions near.
By lavender's calm and cinnamon's might,
Star anise guides me through the night."

4. Apply the Frosting

The Frosting Veil can be used in various ways, depending on your purpose:

- **Edible Application:**
    - Spread the frosting on cookies, cupcakes, or other baked goods. Focus on your intention as you decorate. Consume the treat mindfully before engaging in dream work or meditation.
- **Decorative Ritual:**
    - Use the frosting to decorate a symbolic item, such as a gingerbread star or moon, and place it on your altar as a focus for the spell.
- **Body Anointing:**
    - Place a small amount of the frosting on your third eye (center of your forehead) during meditation to symbolize opening your psychic vision.

5. Perform the Ritual

- If you are focusing on **psychic visions**, sit quietly in a darkened space, light a candle, and focus on the flame. Allow your mind to relax and observe any images or insights that arise.
- If you are focusing on **dream work**, consume the frosted treat or meditate with it on your altar before bed. Visualize the Frosting Veil opening the gateway to vivid, meaningful dreams.

Enhancing the Frosting Veil Spell
1. Incorporate Crystals
Place crystals near the frosting during the spell to amplify its energy:

- **Amethyst:** Enhances intuition and spiritual awareness.
- **Labradorite:** Protects and deepens psychic exploration.
- **Moonstone:** Aligns with lunar energy and supports dream work.

2. Use Incense or Essential Oils
Burn lavender or sandalwood incense, or diffuse essential oils like frankincense or ylang-ylang, to create a calm, meditative atmosphere.

3. Pair with Visualization
While consuming or meditating with the frosting, visualize a shimmering veil parting before you, revealing the spiritual insights, symbols, or messages you seek.

Signs the Spell is Working
After performing the Frosting Veil spell, you may notice:

- Increased vividness and clarity in dreams.
- Heightened intuitive awareness during daily activities.
- Stronger, more frequent flashes of insight or visions during meditation.

- A sense of calm and openness when engaging in spiritual practices.

Maintaining the Energy of the Frosting Veil

- **Revisit Regularly:** Repeat the spell as needed, especially during full moons or times of spiritual exploration.
- **Record Insights:** Keep a dream or vision journal to track your experiences and note any recurring themes or symbols.
- **Cleanse and Recharge:** Periodically cleanse your space and tools with sage or sound to maintain a clear and supportive environment for your work.

Conclusion

The Frosting Veil spell is a creative and powerful ritual for enhancing psychic vision and deepening dream work. By infusing frosting with the magical properties of herbs, spices, and intention, you create a sweet and accessible tool to bridge the gap between the physical and spiritual realms. Whether used for scrying, meditation, or dream exploration, this spell offers a gentle yet potent way to open your intuitive channels and uncover hidden insights.

Chapter 19: Enchanting Gingerbread Familiars

Familiars are magical entities or spiritual allies that assist practitioners in their craft, offering guidance, protection, and energy. **Enchanting Gingerbread Familiars** combines the creativity of crafting with the magical process of imbuing gingerbread figures with energy and intent to serve as temporary magical assistants. These enchanted creations are ideal for tasks such as protection, manifestation, and ritual amplification, and they bring a unique charm to your magical work.

This chapter explores how to craft, enchant, and work with gingerbread familiars, from preparing the dough to animating them with intention.

The Role of Familiars in Magic

Familiars are traditionally viewed as spiritual companions that help practitioners by:

- Amplifying energy during spells or rituals.
- Offering guidance and wisdom.
- Protecting the practitioner from negativity or harm.
- Assisting in specific magical tasks, such as divination or manifestation.

By crafting and enchanting gingerbread familiars, you create a physical vessel through which you can channel your intentions and invite supportive energies to aid in your magical work.

Magical Ingredients for Gingerbread Familiars

Each ingredient in the gingerbread dough carries magical properties, contributing to the power of the familiar:

Base Ingredients

- **Flour:** Represents stability and grounding, providing a solid foundation for the familiar.
- **Sugar:** Adds sweetness and attracts positive energy.
- **Molasses:** Symbolizes resilience and the ability to endure challenges.
- **Eggs:** Represent life force and vitality, imbuing the familiar with energy.

Spices

- **Cinnamon:** Provides warmth, protection, and strength.
- **Ginger:** Adds empowerment and energizes the familiar.
- **Nutmeg:** Invites luck and blessings.
- **Clove:** Seals and strengthens the familiar's magical purpose.

Decorative Elements

- **Icing or Edible Paint:** Use to draw sigils, symbols, or designs to align the familiar with its purpose.
- **Candies or Nuts:** Represent features or enhancements that amplify the familiar's specific abilities.

Tools and Materials

To create and enchant your gingerbread familiar, gather the following:

- Rolling pin and cookie cutters (animal or humanoid shapes are ideal)
- Baking sheet lined with parchment paper
- Ingredients for gingerbread dough (recipe provided below)
- Icing, edible paint, or natural decorations
- A candle (color based on the familiar's intended purpose: white for general, black for protection, green for abundance, etc.)
- A small dish of salt or herbs for cleansing
- Optional: Crystals or charms to place near the familiar for added energy

Crafting the Gingerbread Familiar
Step 1: Prepare the Dough
Ingredients:

- 2 ½ cups all-purpose flour
- 1 teaspoon baking soda
- 1 teaspoon ground cinnamon
- 1 teaspoon ground ginger
- ½ teaspoon ground nutmeg
- ½ teaspoon ground cloves
- ½ cup unsalted butter, softened
- ½ cup dark brown sugar
- 1 egg
- ½ cup molasses

Instructions:

1. In a medium bowl, combine the flour, baking soda, and spices. Set aside.
2. In a separate bowl, cream the butter and brown sugar until light and fluffy. Add the egg and molasses, mixing well.
3. Gradually add the dry ingredients to the wet mixture, stirring until a dough forms.
4. Wrap the dough in plastic wrap and chill for 30 minutes to 1 hour. Use this time to focus on the purpose of your familiar and set your intentions.

Step 2: Shape and Bake

1. Preheat your oven to 350°F (175°C).
2. Roll out the chilled dough on a floured surface to about ¼-inch thickness.
3. Use cookie cutters to create the shape of your familiar. Popular choices include animals (e.g., cats, birds, or foxes) or humanoid figures.
4. Place the shapes on a baking sheet and bake for 10–12 minutes. Allow them to cool completely.

Step 3: Decorate with Purpose

1. Use icing, edible paint, or natural decorations to give your familiar defining features. Add details that symbolize its purpose:
   - Draw protective runes or sigils for a guardian familiar.
   - Use green icing or symbols of abundance for a prosperity familiar.
   - Add a small edible "third eye" for a familiar aiding in divination.
2. As you decorate, focus on infusing the familiar with energy and intention. Visualize it coming to life and fulfilling its role.

Enchanting the Gingerbread Familiar

Once your familiar is crafted, you'll need to animate and empower it. Follow these steps:

Step 1: Create a Sacred Space

- Cleanse the area where you'll work by sprinkling salt, burning incense, or visualizing white light.
- Place the familiar on a small plate or cloth, surrounded by items that amplify its energy (e.g., crystals, candles, or herbs).

Step 2: Light the Candle

- Light a candle that corresponds to the familiar's purpose. For example:
    ○ White for general assistance or purification.
    ○ Black for protection.
    ○ Green for abundance and prosperity.
    ○ Purple for psychic insight.
- Place the candle near the familiar and focus on the flame, visualizing the energy transferring into the gingerbread figure.

Step 3: Speak the Invocation

- Place your hands over the familiar and speak the following (or create your own) incantation:

"By sweetness and spice, I call thee near,
A spirit of aid, to guard and steer.

Gingerbread familiar, bound by my will,
Awaken now, your purpose fulfill."

- As you chant, visualize the familiar glowing with energy, taking on the qualities you've assigned to it.

Step 4: Seal the Spell

- Seal the spell by letting the candle burn for a few minutes while you hold your focus. Drip a small amount of wax near the familiar as a symbolic seal.

Using Your Gingerbread Familiar
1. Assign a Purpose

- Clearly define the role of your familiar. Some examples include:
    - **Guardian Familiar:** Place it near your front door or on an altar for protection.
    - **Manifestation Familiar:** Keep it in your workspace or near a money jar to amplify abundance.
    - **Divination Familiar:** Use it during tarot readings or scrying sessions to enhance clarity.

2. Interact Regularly

- Speak to your familiar or meditate with it to maintain a strong connection. Treat it as a magical ally, not just an object.

3. Dispose Respectfully

- When the familiar's purpose is complete, thank it for its service. Dispose of it respectfully by burying it in the earth, offering it to nature, or burning it in a ritual fire.

Customizing Your Gingerbread Familiar
You can tailor your familiar to specific needs:

- **Add Crystals:** Place small crystals on or near the familiar to enhance its energy (e.g., amethyst for intuition, citrine for abundance).
- **Incorporate Herbs:** Sprinkle protective or empowering herbs into the dough or use them as decoration.
- **Multiple Familiars:** Create a set of familiars for different purposes, such as protection, guidance, and manifestation.

Signs Your Familiar is Active

You may notice the following signs that your gingerbread familiar is working:

- A sense of its presence or energy in the space.
- Positive shifts in the area of your life aligned with its purpose.
- Symbols or synchronicities related to the familiar's role appearing in your daily life.

Conclusion

Enchanting Gingerbread Familiars is a creative and empowering practice that combines the art of crafting with the magic of intention. By shaping, decorating, and animating these edible allies, you create tangible vessels for spiritual energy that can assist you in your magical work. Whether used for protection, manifestation, or divination, these sweet companions remind us of the power of creativity and intention in the magical arts.

Chapter 20: Seasonal Portal Rituals

Seasonal changes bring unique opportunities to align with the cycles of nature and harness their energy for manifestation, transformation, and spiritual growth. **Seasonal Portal Rituals** use gingerbread crafts as symbolic tools to open energetic pathways—portals—through which blessings can flow into your life. These rituals are designed to work in harmony with the natural world, using the sweetness and symbolism of gingerbread to invoke abundance, protection, and spiritual alignment during the holiday season.

This chapter provides detailed guidance on how to craft, empower, and use gingerbread structures—such as doorways, arches, or symbolic portals—as focal points for opening energetic pathways that invite blessings.

The Concept of Energetic Portals

In magical practice, portals represent doorways between different states of being—physical and spiritual, mundane and magical. By creating gingerbread portals and empowering them with intention, you symbolically and energetically open pathways for blessings to enter your life. These rituals can be used to:

- **Manifest Goals:** Direct energy toward your desires, such as abundance, love, or success.
- **Receive Spiritual Guidance:** Open pathways for divine messages, intuition, or ancestral blessings.
- **Align with Seasonal Energy:** Harness the unique energy of the season to create harmony and balance.

Symbolism of Gingerbread Portals

Gingerbread is ideal for creating magical portals because it represents:

- **Transformation:** The act of baking transforms simple ingredients into something meaningful, symbolizing the shift from intention to manifestation.
- **Sweetness:** Attracts positive energy and blessings.
- **Stability:** Provides a solid foundation for building energetic pathways.

Portal Shapes and Their Meanings:

- **Doors:** Represent opportunities and new beginnings.
- **Arches:** Symbolize protection and the flow of energy.
- **Windows:** Offer clarity and insight.
- **Bridges:** Connect different aspects of life or realms.

Magical Ingredients for Gingerbread Portals

Each ingredient in the gingerbread recipe carries symbolic energy to enhance the portal's power:

Base Ingredients

- **Flour:** Stability and grounding.
- **Sugar:** Sweetness and attraction of positive energy.
- **Molasses:** Depth, resilience, and grounding.
- **Eggs:** Creation and vitality.

Spices

- **Cinnamon:** Protection and warmth.
- **Ginger:** Empowerment and energy flow.
- **Nutmeg:** Blessings and prosperity.

- **Clove:** Sealing energy and enhancing focus.

Decorative Elements

- **Icing:** Represents spiritual connection and clarity.
- **Candies:** Symbolize abundance and joy.
- **Sprinkles or Edible Glitter:** Add magical vibrancy and energy.

Tools and Materials

To create and empower your gingerbread portal, you'll need:

- Rolling pin and cookie cutters (or a knife for freehand shaping)
- Baking sheet lined with parchment paper
- Ingredients for gingerbread dough (recipe provided below)
- Icing or edible decorations
- Candles (color based on your intention: green for prosperity, white for clarity, etc.)
- Crystals, herbs, or charms for empowerment

Crafting the Gingerbread Portal
Step 1: Prepare the Dough
Ingredients:

- 3 cups all-purpose flour
- 1 teaspoon baking soda
- 1 teaspoon ground cinnamon
- 1 teaspoon ground ginger
- ½ teaspoon ground nutmeg
- ½ teaspoon ground cloves
- ½ cup unsalted butter, softened
- ½ cup dark brown sugar
- ½ cup molasses
- 1 egg

Instructions:

1. In a medium bowl, combine the flour, baking soda, and spices. Set aside.
2. In a separate bowl, cream the butter and brown sugar until light and fluffy. Add the molasses and egg, mixing well.
3. Gradually add the dry ingredients to the wet mixture, stirring until a dough forms.
4. Wrap the dough in plastic wrap and chill for 30 minutes.

Step 2: Shape and Bake

1. Preheat your oven to 350°F (175°C).
2. Roll out the chilled dough on a floured surface to about ¼-inch thickness.
3. Use cookie cutters or a knife to shape the portal. For example:

- ◦ A **door** with a rounded or rectangular shape.
- ◦ An **arch** formed by cutting out a half-circle.
- ◦ A **bridge** made from multiple pieces.

4. Place the shapes on a baking sheet and bake for 10–12 minutes. Allow them to cool completely.

Step 3: Decorate with Intention

1. Use icing to outline the portal and create symbolic designs, such as runes, sigils, or spiritual symbols.
2. Add candies, sprinkles, or edible glitter to amplify the portal's energy.
3. As you decorate, focus on the portal's purpose and visualize it glowing with light and energy.

Empowering the Gingerbread Portal

Once the portal is crafted, it's time to empower it with magical energy.

Step 1: Cleanse the Space

- Clear your space of negative energy by burning sage, palo santo, or incense. Place the gingerbread portal on your altar or a clean surface.

Step 2: Light the Candles

- Light one or more candles that correspond to your intention. For example:
  - Green for abundance.
  - White for clarity and spiritual connection.
  - Blue for emotional healing.

Step 3: Invoke the Portal's Power

- Place your hands over the portal and visualize it glowing with energy. Speak an incantation, such as:

"Portal of sweetness, crafted with care,
Open the path, blessings to share.
Through this doorway, let energy flow,
Harmony, abundance, let it grow."

Step 4: Add Enhancements

- Surround the portal with crystals or herbs to amplify its energy:
  - **Clear Quartz:** For clarity and amplification.
  - **Amethyst:** For spiritual connection.
  - **Rosemary:** For protection and purification.

◦ **Bay Leaves:** For manifestation.

Using the Gingerbread Portal

The empowered portal can be used in various magical practices:

1. Manifestation Ritual

- Write your desires on a piece of paper and place it beneath the gingerbread portal. Visualize the portal opening and your blessings flowing through it into your life.

2. Blessing Ritual

- Hold the portal in your hands and focus on a specific blessing you wish to receive (e.g., love, prosperity, or peace). Place the portal in a prominent location, such as your altar or dining table, to radiate its energy.

3. Seasonal Alignment

- Use the portal to connect with the energy of the season. For example, during the winter solstice, visualize the portal opening to invite warmth, light, and renewal into your home.

4. Divination Gateway

- Place the portal near your divination tools (e.g., tarot cards or scrying mirrors) to enhance clarity and insight during readings.

Signs the Portal is Active

You may notice the following signs that your gingerbread portal is working:

- A sense of warmth or energy radiating from the portal.

- Positive shifts in the area of life associated with your intention.
- Symbols or synchronicities related to your desire appearing in daily life.

Maintaining the Portal's Energy

- **Revisit the Spell:** Periodically recharge the portal's energy by lighting candles and speaking affirmations.
- **Respectful Disposal:** When the portal has fulfilled its purpose, thank it for its service and dispose of it respectfully, such as by burying it or offering it to nature.

Conclusion

Seasonal Portal Rituals are a creative and meaningful way to open energetic pathways for blessings. By crafting and empowering ginger-bread portals, you combine the transformative power of baking with magical intention, creating a tangible tool for manifestation and spiritual alignment. Whether used for personal goals, seasonal celebrations, or spiritual growth, these sweet creations offer a unique and powerful way to connect with the energy of the season.

Part V: Honoring and Preserving the Gingerbread Golem's Spirit

Chapter 21: Offerings and Devotions

The **Gingerbread Golem**, as a magical construct and spiritual ally, thrives on intentional energy and symbolic gestures. Offering devotions and symbolic gifts strengthens your bond with the Golem, ensuring its continued assistance in protection, guidance, and blessings. Just as you would honor a deity, spirit, or familiar, the Gingerbread Golem requires attention and care to maintain its magical presence and potency.

This chapter explores ways to honor the Gingerbread Golem with offerings, rituals, and devotions, creating a reciprocal relationship that enhances its effectiveness as a spiritual ally.

Why Offer Devotions to the Gingerbread Golem?

The Gingerbread Golem is not merely a magical construct—it embodies the energies of protection, resilience, and seasonal joy. Offering devotions serves several purposes:

- **Energizing the Golem:** Keeps its magical energy active and aligned with your intentions.
- **Strengthening Connection:** Deepens your bond with the Golem, fostering trust and understanding.
- **Reciprocal Exchange:** Honors the Golem's assistance by offering energy or gratitude in return.
- **Seasonal Alignment:** Celebrates the spirit of the holiday season, enhancing its protective and harmonious qualities.

Types of Offerings for the Gingerbread Golem

Offerings can take many forms, from tangible gifts to acts of devotion. Here are some ideas:

1. Food and Drink

Since the Golem is made of gingerbread, edible offerings resonate deeply with its essence:

- **Gingerbread Pieces:** Small pieces of gingerbread or other baked goods serve as symbolic nourishment.
- **Honey or Syrup:** Represents sweetness and gratitude, aligning with the Golem's protective and nurturing qualities.
- **Warm Beverages:** Mulled cider, spiced tea, or hot chocolate invoke the warmth and joy of the season.

2. Seasonal Decorations

Decorations honor the Golem's connection to the festive season:

- **Candles:** White, gold, or green candles symbolize light, abundance, and protection.
- **Evergreens:** Sprigs of pine, cedar, or holly offer grounding and protective energy.
- **Ornaments:** Small, symbolic ornaments can be placed on or near the Golem's altar as tokens of appreciation.

3. Symbolic Gestures

Acts of devotion can be as meaningful as physical offerings:

- **Spoken Gratitude:** Verbally thank the Golem for its assistance and presence.

- **Music or Songs:** Sing or play seasonal songs that align with the Golem's festive nature.
- **Acts of Kindness:** Perform charitable acts in the Golem's name, spreading the protective and generous energy it represents.

Creating an Altar for the Gingerbread Golem

An altar dedicated to the Gingerbread Golem provides a focal point for offerings and devotions. Here's how to set one up:

1. Choose a Sacred Space

- Select a small, clean area where you can safely leave offerings and perform devotions. This could be a table, shelf, or dedicated corner of your home.

2. Place the Golem

- If you've crafted a physical Gingerbread Golem (from earlier chapters), place it at the center of the altar. Alternatively, you can use a symbolic representation, such as a gingerbread cookie, ornament, or drawing.

3. Add Altar Decorations

- Incorporate seasonal decorations that resonate with the Golem's energy:
    - **Candles:** For light and warmth.
    - **Crystals:** Clear quartz (amplification), citrine (abundance), or obsidian (protection).
    - **Herbs and Spices:** Cinnamon sticks, star anise, or dried cloves to align with its essence.

4. Include Offering Space

- Leave space for food, drink, or other offerings you'll present during devotions.

5. Create a Written Connection

- Write down your intentions or gratitude on slips of paper and place them on the altar. These notes act as ongoing reminders of your bond with the Golem.

Rituals of Devotion

Devotional rituals formalize your relationship with the Golem and amplify its energy. Here are some examples:

1. Daily Gratitude Ritual

A simple daily practice to maintain your connection with the Golem.

Steps:

1. Light a candle on the Golem's altar.
2. Place a small offering (e.g., a piece of gingerbread or a sprinkle of cinnamon) on the altar.
3. Speak aloud:

"Gingerbread Golem, ally so true,
Protector of hearth, I honor you.
With sweetness and strength, your blessings flow,
My gratitude deep, your light shall grow."

1. Let the candle burn for a few minutes before extinguishing it.

2. Seasonal Blessing Ritual

A more elaborate ritual to align with the seasonal energy and strengthen the Golem's protective spirit.

What You'll Need:

- A white or gold candle
- A small bowl of honey or syrup
- Cinnamon sticks or dried herbs
- A bell or chime

Steps:

1. Cleanse the altar space with incense or sound (ringing a bell or clapping your hands).
2. Light the candle and place it near the Golem.
3. Dip a cinnamon stick into the honey and draw a protective symbol (such as a circle or pentacle) near the Golem.
4. Speak the following incantation:

"By sweetness and spice, by light and cheer,
I honor the Golem who stands so near.
Protect my space, bring joy to this home,
Blessings abound, wherever you roam."

1. Ring the bell or chime to close the ritual and seal the energy.

3. Offering of Sweet Intentions

This ritual focuses on offering written intentions or prayers to the Golem.

What You'll Need:

- Slips of paper and a pen
- A small dish or jar
- Optional: Gingerbread cookies or candies

Steps:

1. Write down your intentions, wishes, or prayers on the slips of paper.
2. Fold the papers and place them in the dish or jar on the altar.
3. Leave a small edible offering alongside the written intentions.
4. Say:

"Golem of ginger, hear my plea,
Protect and bless, as I honor thee.
Sweet as the treat, strong as your might,
May these intentions take swift flight."

Maintaining Your Devotion

To keep your connection with the Golem strong:

- **Refresh Offerings Regularly:** Replace food offerings before they spoil and rotate decorations to keep the altar vibrant.
- **Acknowledge Its Work:** When you notice the Golem's influence in your life (e.g., protection, harmony, or blessings), express gratitude through devotions or acts of kindness.
- **Seasonal Alignment:** As the seasons change, adapt your offerings and rituals to reflect the energy of the time, ensuring the Golem remains aligned with your intentions.

Signs the Golem is Responding

You may notice these signs that your Gingerbread Golem is actively working as your ally:

- A sense of warmth or presence around its altar.
- Positive shifts in the areas of life you've dedicated to the Golem's protection or blessings.
- Symbols or synchronicities, such as seeing gingerbread or other related imagery unexpectedly.

Respectful Retirement of the Golem

When it's time to retire the Gingerbread Golem, honor it with a respectful farewell:

1. Thank the Golem for its service and express your gratitude.
2. Disassemble the altar and dispose of the Golem respectfully by:
    ◦ Returning it to nature (e.g., burying it).

- Burning it in a ritual fire to release its energy.

3. Speak a closing blessing:

"Gingerbread Golem, your work is done,
I release you now with gratitude spun.
Go in peace, your energy free,
My thanks forever, so mote it be."

Conclusion

Offerings and devotions are integral to honoring the Gingerbread Golem as a spiritual ally. Through intentional acts of gratitude, symbolic offerings, and meaningful rituals, you cultivate a reciprocal relationship that strengthens the Golem's presence in your magical practice. These devotions not only empower the Golem but also deepen your connection to the protective and harmonious energy it represents, enriching your spiritual journey.

Chapter 22: Seasonal Cycles of the Golem

The **Gingerbread Golem**, like all magical constructs tied to nature and the seasons, resonates with the cyclical energies of the Earth. Aligning your rituals with the turning of the seasons allows you to harmonize your practices with these natural rhythms, amplifying the Golem's protective, nurturing, and transformative powers. Each season carries distinct energy that influences the Golem's purpose and the type of magic it can best support.

This chapter explores how to adapt your work with the Gingerbread Golem to the energy of each season, providing detailed guidance on rituals, offerings, and magical tasks that align with the cycles of the year.

The Significance of Seasonal Alignment

Seasonal alignment honors the natural ebb and flow of energy throughout the year:

- **Winter:** Rest, reflection, and fortification.
- **Spring:** Renewal, growth, and manifestation.
- **Summer:** Vitality, abundance, and protection.
- **Autumn:** Harvest, gratitude, and preparation.

By attuning the Golem's rituals and offerings to the unique energy of each season, you deepen your connection to its protective spirit and maximize its effectiveness in supporting your magical intentions.

Winter: Reflection and Fortification

Energy of the Season: Winter represents stillness, introspection, and the strengthening of foundations. It is a time for rest and preparation, as well as fortifying your home and spirit against external challenges.

Focus for the Golem:

- **Protection:** Strengthen the Golem's shielding abilities to guard your home and loved ones.
- **Healing:** Use this time for self-care and emotional fortification.
- **Dream Work:** Deepen your connection to the subconscious through dream rituals.

Offerings and Decorations:

- **Offerings:** Warm beverages like spiced cider, ginger tea, or hot chocolate; evergreen sprigs; and cinnamon sticks.
- **Decorations:** Snowflake symbols, candles, and white or silver accents to reflect the stillness of winter.

Winter Ritual for the Golem:

1. Light a white candle on the Golem's altar to symbolize purity and protection.
2. Offer a small bowl of warm spiced cider or tea.
3. Speak this incantation:

"In winter's stillness, strong you stand,
Protector of hearth, guardian of land.
Shield us from harm, guide us with might,
Fortify our spirits through the longest night."

1. Meditate on the Golem's protective energy surrounding your home like a warm, glowing shield.

Spring: Renewal and Growth

Energy of the Season: Spring brings renewal, growth, and the blossoming of new opportunities. It is a time for planting seeds—both literal and metaphorical—and manifesting your desires.

Focus for the Golem:

- **Manifestation:** Empower the Golem to assist in achieving your goals and nurturing growth.
- **Clearing Obstacles:** Use the Golem's energy to remove lingering negativity or blockages.
- **Reconnection:** Strengthen bonds with loved ones and align with the energy of new beginnings.

Offerings and Decorations:

- **Offerings:** Fresh flowers, honey, and early spring herbs like basil and mint.
- **Decorations:** Green and pastel colors, floral patterns, and symbols of budding life (e.g., eggs, butterflies).

Spring Ritual for the Golem:

1. Place a small potted plant or fresh flowers on the altar as a symbol of growth.
2. Sprinkle a pinch of dried basil or mint around the Golem.
3. Speak this incantation:

"In springtime's bloom, I call to thee,
Nurture my dreams, so they may be.

Gingerbread Golem, strong and true,
Help me create what I pursue."

1. Visualize the Golem infusing your goals with energy and removing any blockages in your path.

Summer: Vitality and Abundance

Energy of the Season: Summer is a time of vitality, celebration, and abundance. The energy is expansive, supporting protective magic, manifestation, and joy.

Focus for the Golem:

- **Strength and Vitality:** Enhance the Golem's protective energy to safeguard your endeavors.
- **Celebration:** Align the Golem with the spirit of joy and gratitude.
- **Abundance:** Use the Golem to attract prosperity and ensure the continued growth of your efforts.

Offerings and Decorations:

- **Offerings:** Seasonal fruits like strawberries or oranges, sunflowers, and refreshing drinks like lemonade or herbal iced tea.
- **Decorations:** Bright colors (yellow, gold, or orange), sun symbols, and floral garlands.

Summer Ritual for the Golem:

1. Light a gold or yellow candle on the altar to represent vitality and abundance.
2. Place a small bowl of seasonal fruits as an offering.
3. Speak this incantation:

"In summer's light, so bold and bright,
Guard my path, both day and night.
Gingerbread Golem, with joy you bring,
Abundance flows through everything."

1. Spend a few moments in gratitude, reflecting on the abundance in your life and visualizing the Golem amplifying this energy.

Autumn: Harvest and Gratitude

Energy of the Season: Autumn is the season of harvest, gratitude, and preparation for the darker months. It's a time to reflect on what you've accomplished, give thanks, and prepare for renewal.

Focus for the Golem:

- **Gratitude:** Honor the Golem's role in your life and the blessings it has helped manifest.
- **Protection:** Prepare for winter by strengthening the Golem's shielding abilities.
- **Release:** Let go of what no longer serves you, creating space for future growth.

Offerings and Decorations:

- **Offerings:** Apples, pumpkins, bread, and seasonal spices like cinnamon and clove.
- **Decorations:** Autumn leaves, cornucopias, and earthy colors (orange, brown, and red).

Autumn Ritual for the Golem:

1. Place a small loaf of bread or an apple on the altar as a harvest offering.
2. Scatter dried autumn leaves around the Golem.

3. Speak this incantation:

"In autumn's glow, with thanks I sing,
To the Golem who guards and blessings bring.
Through harvest time, your power grows,
Protect and guide as the season slows."

1. Reflect on what you've achieved and express gratitude for the Golem's assistance.

Creating a Year-Long Connection

To maintain alignment with the Golem throughout the year:

- **Seasonal Offerings:** Update the altar with offerings and decorations that reflect the energy of the current season.
- **Ritual Adaptation:** Modify rituals to incorporate seasonal elements and intentions.
- **Reflection and Gratitude:** Take time at the end of each season to reflect on the Golem's role in your life and express thanks for its support.

Conclusion

Aligning your rituals with the turning of the seasons enhances your connection to the Gingerbread Golem and deepens its effectiveness as a spiritual ally. By honoring the natural rhythms of the year, you create a harmonious flow of energy that strengthens your magical practice, supports your intentions, and fosters a sense of balance and gratitude. Whether through winter's fortification, spring's renewal, summer's vitality, or autumn's harvest, the Golem stands as a steadfast companion, guiding and protecting you through the cycles of life.

Chapter 23: Repairing a Broken Golem

Even the most well-crafted magical constructs, including the **Gingerbread Golem**, can encounter wear, damage, or spiritual fatigue over time. Whether due to physical cracks in its structure, loss of energy, or overuse in magical work, a broken or weakened Golem needs healing to restore its power. This chapter offers detailed guidance on how to repair or recreate a damaged Gingerbread Golem, ensuring that its protective, nurturing, and magical qualities remain intact.

Understanding the Nature of Damage

Before initiating repairs, assess the type of damage the Golem has sustained:

- **Physical Damage:** Cracks, breaks, or other visible issues in the Golem's gingerbread form.
- **Energetic Weakness:** A sense that the Golem's protective or magical energy has diminished or dissipated.
- **Symbolic Misalignment:** A feeling that the Golem no longer aligns with its original purpose or your intentions.

Each type of damage requires a specific approach to healing, which may involve physical reconstruction, energetic recharging, or symbolic renewal.

Supplies for Repair

Before you begin, gather the following materials to repair or recreate the Golem:

For Physical Repairs

- Edible glue (e.g., royal icing or a sugar syrup)
- Parchment paper or a clean workspace
- Decorations to replace or enhance the original design (optional)

For Energetic Repairs

- Candles (white for general healing, green for renewal, or black for protection)
- Herbs (e.g., rosemary, cinnamon, or lavender for energetic cleansing and empowerment)
- Crystals (e.g., clear quartz, amethyst, or obsidian for charging the Golem)
- Salt or moon water for purification

For Recreation

- Ingredients for making new gingerbread (see recipe in Chapter 18)
- A fresh set of tools for shaping, baking, and decorating

Step-by-Step Guide to Repairing a Broken Golem
1. Cleanse the Golem
Before beginning physical or energetic repairs, cleanse the Golem to remove lingering negativity or stagnant energy:

1. Sprinkle a pinch of salt or lightly brush the Golem with moon water, focusing on clearing away any disruptive energies.
2. Light an incense stick or smudge bundle (e.g., sage, rosemary, or palo santo) and pass the Golem through the smoke while saying:

"By this smoke, I cleanse and renew,
Clearing away what's old, restoring what's true."
2. Repair Physical Damage
Step A: Assess the Breaks

- Examine the Golem for cracks, broken pieces, or other physical damage.
- Determine whether the damage is repairable or if a full reconstruction is necessary.

Step B: Use Edible Glue

- Mix royal icing or sugar syrup to act as an adhesive.
- Gently press broken pieces together and secure them with the glue. Allow it to dry completely before handling.

- If small crumbs or fragments are missing, patch them with extra dough or icing, smoothing the surface as much as possible.

Step C: Redecorate

- Use fresh icing, edible glitter, or other decorations to restore the Golem's appearance. As you decorate, focus on imbuing it with new energy, visualizing it regaining strength and vitality.

3. Recharge the Golem's Energy

Once physical repairs are complete, restore the Golem's magical essence with an energetic recharge:

Step A: Light a Candle

- Place the repaired Golem on your altar or a clean surface.
- Light a candle corresponding to your intention:
    - **White:** General healing and purification.
    - **Green:** Renewal and growth.
    - **Black:** Protective energy.

Step B: Surround with Empowering Elements

- Arrange herbs, crystals, or charms around the Golem to amplify its energy:
    - **Herbs:** Sprinkle dried rosemary or cinnamon around the Golem for protection and strength.
    - **Crystals:** Place clear quartz or amethyst near the Golem to enhance its energetic alignment.
    - **Salt Circle:** Create a protective circle of salt around the Golem to seal in its renewed energy.

Step C: Speak an Invocation

- Place your hands over the Golem and visualize it glowing with a vibrant, healing light. Speak the following (or your own) incantation:

"Golem of ginger, sweet and strong,
Renew your purpose, where you belong.
By spice and flame, I heal and restore,
Your power returns, as it was before."

Step D: Let It Rest

- Allow the Golem to remain undisturbed for 24 hours in a sacred space to absorb the energy of the ritual and solidify its renewed purpose.

Recreating the Golem

If the Golem is too damaged to repair, a complete reconstruction may be necessary. Follow these steps to create a new Gingerbread Golem while honoring the energy of the original:

1. Release the Original Golem

- Thank the original Golem for its service, expressing gratitude for the protection and blessings it provided.
- Dispose of the remains respectfully by:
    - Returning them to nature (e.g., burying them).
    - Burning them in a ritual fire to release their energy.

2. Craft a New Golem

- Follow the recipe and instructions in Chapter 18 to create a fresh Gingerbread Golem.
- Incorporate a small piece of the original Golem (e.g., a crumb or decoration) into the new one to transfer its energy and legacy.

3. Empower the New Golem

- Perform a new empowerment ritual, aligning the Golem with its intended purpose and renewing its protective and magical essence.

Maintaining the Golem's Energy

To prevent future damage and maintain the Golem's strength:

- **Regular Cleansing:** Periodically cleanse the Golem with salt, moon water, or incense to remove stagnant energy.
- **Reinforce with Rituals:** Perform seasonal rituals (as detailed in Chapter 22) to recharge its energy and align it with the cycles of the year.
- **Monitor for Fatigue:** Pay attention to signs that the Golem's energy is weakening, such as a loss of presence or effectiveness in its tasks.

Signs the Golem Is Repaired

You'll know the Golem has been successfully repaired or recreated when:

- You sense its energy is vibrant and active once more.
- It resumes its protective or magical functions effectively.
- You feel a renewed connection and alignment with its presence.

Conclusion

Repairing or recreating a damaged Gingerbread Golem is an opportunity to deepen your bond with this magical ally while reaffirming its purpose in your practice. By addressing physical, energetic, and symbolic aspects of damage, you restore the Golem's power and ensure it continues to serve as a source of protection, guidance, and seasonal joy. This process not only heals the Golem but also reinforces the cyclical nature of magic, reminding us that renewal and transformation are integral to every magical path.

Chapter 24: The Legacy of Sweet Magicks

Traditions involving the **Gingerbread Golem** are steeped in creativity, seasonal joy, and the transformative power of magic. Passing down these traditions ensures that the wisdom of **Sweet Magicks** continues to inspire and empower future generations. Whether shared with family, friends, or a broader magical community, these practices nurture connection, spark imagination, and infuse the holiday season with spiritual meaning.

This chapter explores how to preserve and share the legacy of Gingerbread Golem traditions, offering guidance on teaching, storytelling, and creating lasting rituals that honor this unique magical practice.

The Importance of Passing Down Sweet Magicks

Sharing the legacy of Gingerbread Golem traditions serves several purposes:

- **Preservation of Knowledge:** Ensures that the wisdom of Sweet Magicks is not lost but evolves over time.
- **Building Connection:** Fosters bonds among family, friends, and communities by engaging in meaningful rituals.
- **Inspiring Creativity:** Encourages others to explore and adapt the traditions to their unique spiritual or cultural practices.
- **Seasonal Alignment:** Aligns participants with the deeper meanings of the season, such as gratitude, protection, and abundance.

The Core Elements of Gingerbread Golem Traditions

To effectively pass down these practices, focus on the following core elements:

1. Storytelling

The narrative of the Gingerbread Golem is central to its tradition. Sharing its origins, purpose, and magical symbolism provides context and meaning for others.

2. Ritual Practices

Teach the foundational rituals of creating, empowering, and working with Gingerbread Golems. Emphasize the spiritual significance behind each step, from crafting to empowerment.

3. Seasonal Cycles

Explain how the Golem's energy aligns with the turning of the seasons, as discussed in Chapter 22. Highlight how these cycles can inspire ongoing rituals and devotions.

4. Creativity and Adaptation

Encourage those you teach to adapt the traditions to their unique needs and intentions. Sweet Magicks are inherently flexible, allowing for personalization and innovation.

Sharing the Gingerbread Golem Legacy

There are many ways to pass down this magical tradition, from intimate family gatherings to workshops and community celebrations.

1. Family Rituals

Create annual family traditions centered on the Gingerbread Golem:

- **Seasonal Crafting:** Host a family gathering to bake and decorate Gingerbread Golems, teaching children and adults alike the significance of each step.
- **Storytime and Magic:** Share the story of the Golem as part of a seasonal storytelling ritual, weaving in lessons about protection, gratitude, and creativity.
- **Altar Building:** Invite family members to participate in setting up a Gingerbread Golem altar, contributing offerings and decorations that reflect their intentions for the season.

2. Community Workshops

Host workshops or gatherings to teach others about Gingerbread Golem traditions:

- **Crafting Classes:** Offer hands-on classes in baking and decorating Gingerbread Golems, incorporating the magical symbolism behind the process.
- **Seasonal Rituals:** Lead group rituals that empower participants' creations and align them with seasonal energies.
- **Storytelling Sessions:** Share myths, legends, and personal anecdotes about the Gingerbread Golem to inspire connection and understanding.

3. Written and Visual Guides

Preserve the tradition in written or visual formats to share with a broader audience:

- **Books and Manuals:** Compile the rituals, recipes, and magical practices associated with the Gingerbread Golem into a guidebook or family grimoire.
- **Online Tutorials:** Create videos or blog posts demonstrating how to craft, empower, and use Gingerbread Golems in magical practice.
- **Artistic Expressions:** Use illustrations, photography, or other artistic mediums to convey the magic and beauty of Sweet Magicks.

4. Personalized Gifts

Use Gingerbread Golems as meaningful, magical gifts:

- **Custom Golems:** Craft Golems personalized for the recipient, aligning them with their specific needs or intentions (e.g., protection, abundance, or emotional healing).
- **Spell Kits:** Assemble kits with instructions, ingredients, and tools for creating a Gingerbread Golem, encouraging recipients to engage in the tradition themselves.
- **Blessed Baked Goods:** Prepare gingerbread cookies or cakes imbued with blessings and share them as part of your seasonal celebrations.

Teaching the Rituals: Step-by-Step
1. The Story of the Gingerbread Golem
Start with the narrative. For example:

- Share the myth of how the Gingerbread Golem was first created to protect homes during the harshness of winter.
- Explain its role as a guardian, guide, and symbol of seasonal joy and resilience.

2. The Crafting Process
Demonstrate the step-by-step process of creating a Gingerbread Golem:

1. **Mixing the Dough:** Highlight the magical symbolism of each ingredient (e.g., flour for stability, spices for protection).
2. **Shaping the Golem:** Discuss the significance of the Golem's form and encourage creative designs.
3. **Decorating:** Teach how to use symbols, runes, or patterns to align the Golem with specific intentions.

3. Empowering the Golem
Guide participants through the ritual of imbuing the Golem with energy:

- Explain how to cleanse the space and focus their intentions.
- Lead them in a spoken or written invocation to animate the Golem.
- Share tips for working with the Golem, such as using it for protection, blessings, or manifestation.

4. Seasonal and Ongoing Practices

Teach how to integrate the Golem into seasonal rituals, daily devotions, or specific magical workings:

- Show how to align the Golem's purpose with seasonal energies.
- Encourage regular offerings and gratitude rituals to maintain the Golem's energy.

Creating a Legacy: The Role of Documentation

Documenting your Gingerbread Golem traditions ensures that they endure for generations. Consider the following methods:

1. Family Grimoire

Compile your rituals, recipes, and personal stories into a family grimoire or magical cookbook. Include:

- Instructions for creating and empowering Gingerbread Golems.
- Seasonal correspondences and rituals.
- Personal anecdotes or reflections on how the Golem has supported your magical practice.

2. Digital Archives

Use digital tools to preserve and share the tradition:

- Create a website or social media page dedicated to Sweet Magicks.
- Record video tutorials or live-stream workshops to engage a wider audience.
- Share recipes, spells, and tips through email newsletters or downloadable PDFs.

3. Storybooks and Art

Turn the Gingerbread Golem's story into a children's book, illustrated guide, or piece of art. These mediums are particularly effective for teaching young audiences while preserving the tradition's charm and magic.

Encouraging Innovation in Sweet Magicks

While it's essential to preserve the core elements of the Gingerbread Golem tradition, encourage those you teach to innovate and make it their own:

- **New Ingredients:** Experiment with different spices, decorations, or baking methods to reflect unique cultural or personal influences.
- **Modern Applications:** Adapt the Golem's purpose to contemporary needs, such as digital protection or emotional healing.
- **Collaborative Rituals:** Work with others to create new group practices, combining traditional elements with fresh ideas.

Signs of a Thriving Legacy

You'll know the Gingerbread Golem tradition is thriving when:

- Participants share their personal stories or adaptations of the practice.
- New generations express excitement and creativity in engaging with Sweet Magicks.
- The tradition evolves organically while preserving its magical essence.

Conclusion

The legacy of **Sweet Magicks** lies in its ability to inspire, connect, and empower those who embrace it. By teaching the rituals, sharing the stories, and encouraging creativity, you ensure that the Gingerbread

Golem continues to bring protection, joy, and magic to future generations. Whether through family traditions, community workshops, or artistic expressions, the Gingerbread Golem serves as a timeless symbol of resilience, warmth, and the transformative power of seasonal magic.

Chapter 25: The Final Feast Ritual

The **Final Feast Ritual** is a culminating ceremony in the Gingerbread Golem tradition. This spell represents the closing of a magical cycle, allowing the practitioner to symbolically absorb the Golem's blessings, protection, and energies into their life. As the Golem's purpose reaches its conclusion, the act of consuming it transforms its physical and magical essence into personal empowerment and abundance.

This chapter provides an in-depth guide to preparing, performing, and closing the Final Feast Ritual. It is a celebration of gratitude, transformation, and the cyclical nature of magic.

The Purpose of the Final Feast Ritual

The Final Feast Ritual serves multiple purposes:

- **Absorbing the Golem's Energy:** The ritual transfers the blessings, protection, and intentions infused into the Golem into the practitioner's life.
- **Closing the Cycle:** It honors the Golem's service and concludes its role in a meaningful and respectful way.
- **Celebration and Gratitude:** The feast is a joyful acknowledgment of the magic and blessings the Golem has brought into your life.

When to Perform the Final Feast Ritual

The ritual is best performed:

- At the end of a magical cycle, such as the turning of a season or the fulfillment of an intention.
- During a significant moment of transition, such as the New Year, a solstice, or a personal milestone.
- When the Golem's energy has completed its purpose and is ready to be released.

Preparations for the Ritual
1. Cleanse Your Space

- Purify the ritual area with incense, salt, or moon water to create a sacred space.
- Place the Golem on a clean plate or platter, surrounded by decorative or magical items such as candles, crystals, or herbs.

2. Gather Supplies

- The Gingerbread Golem: Fully intact or repaired if necessary.
- Candles: White for purification, gold for blessings, or green for prosperity.
- Additional Food and Drink: Complementary items for the feast, such as spiced tea, cider, or fresh fruit.
- A knife or small utensil: For cutting or breaking the Golem during the ritual.
- A journal or notebook: To record reflections and insights after the ritual.

3. Set Your Intentions

- Reflect on the Golem's purpose and the blessings it has brought. Write down your intentions for absorbing these energies, such as:
    - Protection for your home or family.
    - Abundance in your personal or professional life.
    - Healing, guidance, or emotional support.

Creating the Ritual Space

Set up a sacred space that reflects the energy of the ritual:

- **Altar Layout:** Place the Golem at the center of the altar, with candles, crystals, or seasonal decorations surrounding it.
- **Lighting:** Dim the lights and use candles to create a warm, sacred atmosphere.
- **Symbols of Gratitude:** Incorporate items that represent the blessings or intentions tied to the Golem, such as coins for abundance, feathers for guidance, or flowers for gratitude.

Performing the Final Feast Ritual
1. Opening the Ritual

1. Light a candle to symbolize the beginning of the ritual and the illumination of the Golem's blessings.
2. Speak an opening invocation to call upon the Golem's spirit and
   the energies it represents. For example:

"Golem of ginger, sweet and wise,
Your blessings I honor, beneath the skies.
As we gather, this feast we share,
Your magic flows through the love and care."

2. Expressing Gratitude

1. Take a moment to reflect on the Golem's purpose and the ways it
   has supported you.
2. Speak aloud your gratitude for its protection, guidance, and blessings. You might say:

"I thank you for your strength and grace,
For guarding my home, this sacred space.
Your service is honored, your work is done,
Your energy flows to everyone."

3. Transferring the Energy

1. Place your hands over the Golem and visualize its energy glowing
   warmly, radiating the intentions and blessings it holds.
2. Speak an incantation to transfer its energy into yourself and your
   life:

"From form to spirit, from spice to flame,
Your blessings I take, your gifts remain.

Through this feast, your magic flows,
Into my life, where it grows and grows."

4. The Feast

1. Carefully cut or break the Golem into pieces, focusing on the transfer of energy from the physical form into your being.
2. Share the pieces with others participating in the ritual, or consume them yourself if working alone.
3. As you eat, savor each bite mindfully, visualizing the Golem's blessings being absorbed into your body, mind, and spirit.

5. Optional Additions

- **Seasonal Drinks:** Sip on a warm beverage, such as spiced cider or tea, to complement the Golem's sweetness and enhance the ritual's warmth.
- **Affirmations:** Speak affirmations aligned with the Golem's purpose as you eat. For example:
  - *"I am protected and secure."*
  - *"Abundance flows into my life with ease."*
  - *"I welcome love, joy, and harmony."*

Closing the Ritual
1. Release the Golem's Spirit

1. Light a second candle (black for closure or white for purification) to symbolize the Golem's release.
2. Speak a farewell blessing:

"Gingerbread Golem, your journey ends,
Your magic remains, as love transcends.
I release you now, your task complete,
Your blessings flow, your spirit sweet."

2. Final Cleansing

1. Cleanse the space with incense, sound, or a sprinkling of salt to clear any residual energy.
2. Extinguish the candles, symbolizing the closing of the ritual.

After the Ritual
Reflect and Record

Take a few moments to journal your thoughts, feelings, and insights from the ritual. Consider:

- How did the Golem's energy impact your life?
- What blessings or intentions do you feel are now integrated into your being?
- How do you plan to carry these energies forward?

Commemorate the Golem

If you wish, keep a small token from the ritual, such as a decoration or a crumb from the Golem, as a reminder of its blessings.

Adapting the Final Feast Ritual

The Final Feast Ritual can be adapted to suit your unique needs:

- **Community Rituals:** Involve family or friends in the ritual, with each participant sharing their reflections on the Golem's blessings.
- **Alternative Offerings:** If consuming the Golem isn't feasible, bury it in nature as an offering to the Earth, symbolizing the return of its energy to the cycle of life.
- **Personalization:** Tailor the incantations, decorations, or offerings to align with your spiritual practice or cultural traditions.

The Symbolism of the Final Feast

The Final Feast Ritual is a powerful reminder of the cyclical nature of magic and life:

- It transforms the Golem from a physical protector into an internalized source of strength and energy.
- It honors the interconnectedness of creation, transformation, and renewal.
- It celebrates the sweetness of life, the power of intention, and the enduring legacy of magical traditions.

Conclusion

The **Final Feast Ritual** is the culmination of the Gingerbread Golem's journey, transforming its essence into a source of personal empowerment and blessings. By mindfully absorbing its energy, you honor its service while embracing the magic it has infused into your life. This ritual is not just a conclusion but a beginning—an opportunity to carry the Golem's legacy forward as you step into a new cycle of growth, gratitude, and transformation.

Appendices

Appendix I: Magical Recipes and Ingredients

This appendix serves as a comprehensive reference for the magical ingredients and tools used throughout the book. Each ingredient is listed with its magical properties, practical applications, and possible substitutions. Whether you are crafting a Gingerbread Golem, performing a ritual, or preparing offerings, this guide ensures you have the knowledge and flexibility to work with what you have while preserving the intended magical essence.

Common Magical Ingredients

Flour

- Magical Properties: Stability, grounding, the foundation of intentions.
- Applications: Used in crafting the base of the Gingerbread Golem and other baked goods.
- Substitutions: Almond flour (adds an element of prosperity) or oat flour (symbolizes nurturing and protection).

Sugar

- Magical Properties: Sweetness, attraction of positive energy, joy, and lightness.
- Applications: Sweetening spells, binding rituals, and baked goods.
- Substitutions: Honey (for longevity and divine connection), agave syrup (for fluid energy), or coconut sugar (for grounding sweetness).

Molasses

- **Magical Properties**: Depth, resilience, patience, and grounding.
- **Applications**: Strengthening the magical foundation of the Golem and rituals focused on resilience.
- **Substitutions**: Dark honey or maple syrup (both provide similar grounding and enriching qualities).

Eggs

- **Magical Properties**: Vitality, creation, fertility, and the birth of new energy.
- **Applications**: Symbolic of life force in baking and manifestation rituals.
- **Substitutions**: Flaxseed or chia seed gel (symbolizes resourcefulness and adaptation) for vegan practices.

Butter

- **Magical Properties**: Abundance, nourishment, richness, and physical grounding.
- **Applications**: Used in dough to symbolize luxury and sustenance.
- **Substitutions**: Coconut oil (adds a tropical energy and emotional warmth) or vegan margarine.

Magical Spices
Cinnamon

- **Magical Properties:** Protection, warmth, passion, prosperity, and amplification of magical energy.
- **Applications:** Incorporated into the Golem and rituals for energy and protection.
- **Substitutions:** Cardamom (adds a gentle warmth and focus) or ginger (enhances fiery energy).

Ginger

- **Magical Properties:** Empowerment, courage, energy, and manifestation.
- **Applications:** Strengthening spells, enhancing the vitality of magical constructs.
- **Substitutions:** Turmeric (for grounding and inner strength) or allspice (for added intensity).

Nutmeg

- **Magical Properties:** Luck, prosperity, blessings, and spiritual insight.
- **Applications:** Used in manifestation spells and rituals for attracting abundance.
- **Substitutions:** Mace (closely related to nutmeg) or clove (adds depth and intensity).

Clove

- Magical Properties: Protection, banishment of negativity, sealing magical intentions.
- Applications: Enhancing protective spells and sealing rituals.
- Substitutions: Star anise (for clarity and spiritual focus) or black pepper (for protection and banishment).

Vanilla

- Magical Properties: Harmony, love, emotional healing, and spiritual connection.
- Applications: Adding warmth and unity to magical recipes and rituals.
- Substitutions: Rose water (for love and emotional healing) or almond extract (for blessings and abundance).

Herbs and Plants
Rosemary

- **Magical Properties:** Protection, purification, remembrance, and clarity.
- **Applications:** Used in cleansing rituals and for maintaining focus in magical work.
- **Substitutions:** Thyme (for purification and courage) or sage (for cleansing and grounding).

Lavender

- **Magical Properties:** Peace, relaxation, dream enhancement, and intuitive insight.
- **Applications:** Incorporated in dream work, meditation, and rituals for emotional balance.
- **Substitutions:** Chamomile (for calm and clarity) or mint (for mental renewal and refreshment).

Peppermint

- **Magical Properties:** Clarity, renewal, healing, and mental stimulation.
- **Applications:** Refreshing energy for focus and spiritual cleansing.
- **Substitutions:** Spearmint (similar properties but milder) or eucalyptus (for clarity and purification).

Sacred Resins and Oils
Frankincense

- **Magical Properties:** Purification, spiritual elevation, divine connection, and protection.
- **Applications:** Used in incense for rituals and empowerment ceremonies.
- **Substitutions:** Copal resin (for purification and spiritual clarity) or myrrh (for grounding and divine connection).

Myrrh

- **Magical Properties:** Grounding, protection, healing, and resilience.
- **Applications:** Enhances stability and spiritual focus in rituals.
- **Substitutions:** Dragon's blood resin (for powerful protection and sealing) or patchouli (for grounding and abundance).

Orange Oil

- **Magical Properties:** Joy, abundance, vitality, and renewal.
- **Applications:** Infused in oils for prosperity and happiness rituals.
- **Substitutions:** Lemon oil (for clarity and purification) or grapefruit oil (for energizing and uplifting energy).

Magical Tools and Substitutions
Candles

- **Magical Properties:** Represent fire, transformation, and illumination.
- **Applications:** Central to rituals for focus and energy.
- **Substitutions:** LED candles for flame-free environments, or small bowls of salt water for reflective energy.

Crystals

- **Magical Properties:** Amplify and focus energy, aligned with specific intentions.
  - **Clear Quartz:** Amplification and clarity.
  - **Amethyst:** Spiritual insight and protection.
  - **Citrine:** Abundance and confidence.
  - **Obsidian:** Grounding and banishment of negativity.
- **Substitutions:** Stones from nature (cleansed with intent) or metallic objects (e.g., coins for abundance, keys for clarity).

Incense

- **Magical Properties:** Cleanse, purify, and invoke specific energies depending on the scent.
- **Applications:** Used to cleanse spaces and empower rituals.
- **Substitutions:** Essential oil diffusers, or dried herbs burned safely (e.g., rosemary, thyme, or bay leaves).

Essential Magical Recipes
Basic Royal Icing (Edible Glue)

- Ingredients: 1 cup powdered sugar, 1–2 tablespoons milk, ½ teaspoon vanilla extract.
- Magical Properties: Binding, unity, and sealing.
- Uses: Repairs and decorates the Gingerbread Golem.

Sweet Energy Tea

- Ingredients: 1 teaspoon cinnamon, 1 teaspoon ginger, 1 teaspoon honey, and 1 cup boiling water.
- Magical Properties: Vitality, protection, and grounding.
- Uses: Drunk during rituals to align with the Golem's energy.

Seasonal Spiced Incense

- Ingredients: Equal parts cinnamon, clove, and rosemary.
- Magical Properties: Protection, purification, and seasonal alignment.
- Uses: Burned during rituals to cleanse and empower the space.

Tips for Substitution

- Intention First: When substituting, focus on the intention behind the ingredient or tool to maintain the ritual's energy.

- **Combine Similar Energies:** Pair two similar ingredients to replicate the missing element (e.g., cinnamon and nutmeg together for warmth and prosperity).
- **Personalize Your Magic:** Feel free to adapt ingredients based on what resonates with your own energy or cultural background.

Conclusion

This appendix offers a detailed and adaptable guide to the magical ingredients and tools used throughout the Gingerbread Golem tradition. Whether you're crafting a Golem, empowering a ritual, or sharing the magic with others, this resource ensures you can create meaningful and powerful practices with confidence, flexibility, and intention.

Appendix II: Chants, Sigils, and Symbols

This appendix provides a detailed collection of **chants**, **sigils**, and **symbols** used throughout the book, as well as templates and instructions for creating personalized sigils for your **Gingerbread Golem**. These magical tools are integral to empowering your rituals, focusing your intentions, and deepening your connection to the Golem's energy.

Chants for Rituals and Spells

Chants are powerful tools for focusing energy, invoking protection, and amplifying magical intent. Below is a collection of chants organized by purpose:

Chants for Empowering the Golem

General Empowerment:

"By spice and flame, I give you life,
Protector of home, banisher of strife.
Gingerbread Golem, strong and true,
Your magic awakens, your purpose imbues."

Protection:

"Guardian of hearth, shield and ward,
By sweetness and strength, this space you guard.
Let no harm cross this sacred line,
With your power, all is fine."

Manifestation:

"From dough to life, from thought to form,
Bring forth blessings in every storm.
Gingerbread Golem, manifest my need,
Empower my path, plant the seed."

Chants for Seasonal Alignment
Winter Solstice:
"In winter's night, your flame shines bright,
Protector of warmth through the longest night.
Golem of spice, keep us whole,
Shield this home, body, and soul."

Spring Renewal:
"By bloom and bud, by earth's new birth,
Bring renewal to this sacred hearth.
Golem of ginger, strong and pure,
Empower new growth, intentions secure."

Summer Abundance:
"In summer's light, your strength does grow,
Abundance flows where your energy goes.
Golem of life, by fire and sun,
Protect and bless, all harm undone."

Autumn Gratitude:
"As leaves do fall, and harvests reap,
Your blessings, Golem, we vow to keep.
Guard us now as the seasons wane,
Until light returns to us again."

Common Sigils for the Golem

Sigils are visual symbols created from magical intentions. They serve as focal points for energy and can be drawn or etched onto the Golem's surface using icing, edible paint, or carved patterns.

Protection Sigil

A simple sigil designed to protect your home and loved ones.

- **Construction:** Start with a circle (representing protection and boundaries) and overlay it with crossed lines to symbolize warding.
- **Application:** Draw this sigil on the Golem's chest or base to enhance its shielding energy.

```
o
/|\
/ | \
/ | \
\_|_/
/ \
```

Abundance Sigil

This sigil attracts prosperity and positive energy into your space.

- **Construction:** Combine a spiral (growth and flow) with an upward-pointing triangle (manifestation and abundance).
- **Application:** Place this sigil on the Golem's hands or feet to symbolize the active gathering of blessings.

```
Δ
/|\
( @ )
```

Guidance Sigil

Use this sigil to enhance the Golem's ability to guide and protect during spiritual or emotional challenges.

- **Construction:** Begin with an eye shape (insight and awareness) and add radiating lines to symbolize clarity and wisdom.
- **Application:** Draw this sigil on the Golem's head or forehead.

```
\ /
--o--
/ \
```

Templates for Personalized Sigils

Creating personalized sigils is an empowering way to align your Golem with specific intentions. Below are templates and instructions to help you craft your own:

Step 1: Define Your Intention

- Write a clear, concise statement of your goal. For example:
    - *"I am protected."*
    - *"Abundance flows into my life."*
    - *"I receive guidance and clarity."*

Step 2: Remove Repeating Letters

- Eliminate all duplicate letters from your intention. For example:
    - *"I am protected"* → *IAMPROTCTD.*

Step 3: Create a Symbol

- Combine the remaining letters into a single, cohesive design. Let your intuition guide you as you arrange the letters into shapes, lines, or patterns. Simplify until the sigil feels powerful and meaningful.

Step 4: Empower the Sigil

- Hold the sigil in your hands and visualize your intention flowing into it. Chant an incantation, such as:

"By line and curve, my will I bind,
This sigil reflects my magical mind."

Visual Symbols and Decorations

Symbols drawn or placed on the Golem enhance its magical focus. Below are examples of universal magical symbols and their meanings:

Runes and Universal Symbols

1. **Pentacle (Protection and Balance):**
   - Drawn on the Golem's chest or base for balance and universal harmony.

1. **Triskelion (Growth and Motion):**
   - Representing cycles of life, place this on the Golem to enhance adaptability and resilience.

1. **Infinity Symbol (Endless Energy):**
   - Drawn to signify ongoing protection and continuous blessings.

∞

Application Techniques

- **Icing and Edible Paint:** Use contrasting colors for clarity when decorating the Golem.
- **Carving Patterns:** Lightly etch symbols into the Golem's dough before baking for an integrated look.
- **Herbs and Spices:** Sprinkle powdered cinnamon, nutmeg, or edible glitter over symbols to empower them further.

Incorporating Chants and Sigils Together

To combine chants and sigils for maximum potency:

1. **Focus:** Place the Golem on your altar and light a candle.
2. **Trace the Sigil:** Using your finger or a decorating tool, trace the sigil onto the Golem while visualizing its energy activating.
3. **Speak the Chant:** Recite the corresponding chant aloud, focusing on the Golem absorbing the sigil's energy and intention.

Conclusion

This appendix equips you with a library of **chants**, **sigils**, and visual symbols to enrich your magical work with the Gingerbread Golem. Whether you're empowering the Golem, aligning it with the seasons, or tailoring it to specific intentions, these tools offer a versatile and creative way to deepen your practice. By combining visualization, sound, and symbolism, you bring your magical intentions to life, ensuring the Golem serves as a powerful and personalized ally in your spiritual journey.

<u>Message from the Author:</u>

I hope you enjoyed this book, I love astrology and knew there was not a book such as this out on the shelf. I love metaphysical items as well. Please check out my other books:

-Life of Government Benefits

-My life of Hell

-My life with Hydrocephalus

-Red Sky

-World Domination:Woman's rule

-World Domination:Woman's Rule 2: The War

-Life and Banishment of Apophis: book 1

-The Kidney Friendly Diet

-The Ultimate Hemp Cookbook

-Creating a Dispensary(legally)

-Cleanliness throughout life: the importance of showering from childhood to adulthood.

-Strong Roots: The Risks of Overcoddling children

-Hemp Horoscopes: Cosmic Insights and Earthly Healing

- Celestial Hemp Navigating the Zodiac: Through the Green Cosmos

-Astrological Hemp: Aligning The Stars with Earth's Ancient Herb

-The Astrological Guide to Hemp: Stars, Signs, and Sacred Leaves

-Green Growth: Innovative Marketing Strategies for your Hemp Products and Dispensary

-Cosmic Cannabis

-Astrological Munchies

-Henry The Hemp

-Zodiacal Roots: The Astrological Soul Of Hemp

- **Green Constellations: Intersection of Hemp and Zodiac**

-Hemp in The Houses: An astrological Adventure Through The Cannabis Galaxy

-Galactic Ganja Guide

Heavenly Hemp

Zodiac Leaves

Doctor Who Astrology

Cannastrology

Stellar Satvias and Cosmic Indicas

Celestial Cannabis: A Zodiac Journey

AstroHerbology: The Sky and The Soil: Volume 1

AstroHerbology:Celestial Cannabis:Volume 2

Cosmic Cannabis Cultivation

The Starry Guide to Herbal Harmony: Volume 1

The Starry Guide to Herbal Harmony: Cannabis Universe: Volume 2

Yugioh Astrology: Astrological Guide to Deck, Duels and more

Nightmare Mansion: Echoes of The Abyss

Nightmare Mansion 2: Legacy of Shadows

Nightmare Mansion 3: Shadows of the Forgotten

Nightmare Mansion 4: Echoes of the Damned

The Life and Banishment of Apophis: Book 2

Nightmare Mansion: Halls of Despair

Healing with Herb: Cannabis and Hydrocephalus

Planetary Pot: Aligning with Astrological Herbs: Volume 1

Fast Track to Freedom: 30 Days to Financial Independence Using AI, Assets, and Agile Hustles

Cosmic Hemp Pathways

How to Become Financially Free in 30 Days: 10,000 Paths to Prosperity

Zodiacal Herbage: Astrological Insights: Volume 1

Nightmare Mansion: Whispers in the Walls

The Daleks Invade Atlantis

Henry the hemp and Hydrocephalus

10X The Kidney Friendly Diet

Cannabis Universe: Adult coloring book

Hemp Astrology: The Healing Power of the Stars

Zodiacal Herbage: Astrological Insights: Cannabis Universe: Volume 2

<u>Planetary Pot: Aligning with Astrological Herbs: Cannabis Universes: Volume 2</u>

Doctor Who Meets the Replicators and SG-1: The Ultimate Battle for Survival

Nightmare Mansion: Curse of the Blood Moon

<u>The Celestial Stoner: A Guide to the Zodiac</u>

Cosmic Pleasures: Sex Toy Astrology for Every Sign

Hydrocephalus Astrology: Navigating the Stars and Healing Waters

Lapis and the Mischievous Chocolate Bar

Celestial Positions: Sexual Astrology for Every Sign

Apophis's Shadow Work Journal: : A Journey of Self-Discovery and Healing

Kinky Cosmos: Sexual Kink Astrology for Every Sign

Digital Cosmos: The Astrological Digimon Compendium

Stellar Seeds: The Cosmic Guide to Growing with Astrology

Apophis's Daily Gratitude Journal

Cat Astrology: Feline Mysteries of the Cosmos

The Cosmic Kama Sutra: An Astrological Guide to Sexual Positions

Unleash Your Potential: A Guided Journal Powered by AI Insights

Whispers of the Enchanted Grove

Cosmic Pleasures: An Astrological Guide to Sexual Kinks

369, 12 Manifestation Journal

Whisper of the nocturne journal(blank journal for writing or drawing)

The Boogey Book

Locked In Reflection: A Chastity Journey Through Locktober

Generating Wealth Quickly:

How to Generate $100,000 in 24 Hours

Star Magic: Harness the Power of the Universe

The Flatulence Chronicles: A Fart Journal for Self-Discovery

The Doctor and The Death Moth

Seize the Day: A Personal Seizure Tracking Journal

The Ultimate Boogeyman Safari: A Journey into the Boogie World and Beyond

Whispers of Samhain: 1,000 Spells of Love, Luck, and Lunar Magic: Samhain Spell Book

Apophis's guides:

Witch's Spellbook Crafting Guide for Halloween

<u>Frost & Flame: The Enchanted Yule Grimoire of 1000 Winter Spells</u>

<u>The Ultimate Boogey Goo Guide & Spooky Activities for Halloween Fun</u>

Harmony of the Scales: A Libra's Spellcraft for Balance and Beauty

The Enchanted Advent: 36 Days of Christmas Wonders

Nightmare Mansion: The Labyrinth of Screams

Harvest of Enchantment: 1,000 Spells of Gratitude, Love, and Fortune for Thanksgiving

The Boogey Chronicles: A Journal of Nightly Encounters and Shadowy Secrets

The 12 Days of Financial Freedom: A Step-by-Step Christmas Countdown to Transform Your Finances

Sigil of the Eternal Spiral Blank Journal

A Christmas Feast: Timeless Recipes for Every Meal

Cosmic Sales: The Astrological Guide to Black Friday Shopping
Legends of the Corn Mother and Other Harvest Myths
Whispers of the Harvest: The Corn Mother's Journal
The Evergreen Spellbook
The Doctor Meets the Boogeyman
The White Witch of Rose Hall's SpellBook
The Gingerbread Golem's Shadow: A Study in Sweet Darkness
The Gingerbread Golem Codex: An Academic Exploration of Sweet Myths

If you want solar for your home go here: https://www.harborsolar.live/apophisenterprises/

Get Some Tarot cards: https://www.makeplayingcards.com/sell/
apophis-occult-shop

Get some shirts: https://www.bonfire.com/store/apophis-shirt-emporium/

Instagrams:
@apophis_enterprises,
@apophisbookemporium,
@apophisscardshop
Twitter: @apophisenterpr1 ,Tiktok:@apophisenterprise
Youtube: @sg1fan23477, @FiresideRetreatKingdom
Hive: @sg1fan23477
CheeLee: @SG1fan23477

Podcast: Apophis Chat Zone: https://open.spotify.com/show/
5zXbrCLEV2xzCp8ybrfHsk?si=fb4d4fdbdce44dec

 –

Newsletter: https://apophiss-newsletter-27c897.beehiiv.com/